VERTICAL LIVING

Compact Architecture for Urban Spaces

gestalten

CONTENTS

THERE'S NO ONE-SIZE-FITS-ALL SOLUTION TO DENSITY

In our growing cities, architects face the challenge of building more homes in increasingly smaller spaces.

When we debate whether or not to densify our cities, perhaps the more important question to ask is: how?

Densification asks us to design buildings that uniquely fit a local context. The "International Style" of cheap reproduction with concrete cores and curtain wall facades took our cities by storm. This style uniformed our cities that once were so unique—London, Vancouver, Shanghai—and killed local traditions and construction knowledge. It often feels like we see the same kind of buildings everywhere.

A sustainable densification is more than efficiency, productivity, and technology. Sustainability starts where we, as residents, care about the buildings we live in. That means that we should be able to identify ourselves within our buildings. Buildings that refer to a local context, a local climate, and a local culture. Buildings that connect directly to our emotions, feelings, and well-being. Buildings that are not separate from their surroundings, but are an integral part of a healthy neighborhood.

This takes ingenuity, and cities don't always give architects a lot of space to work with—awkwardly tiny plots, narrow slivers of land, or sometimes just the roof of another building. The architects in this book all created a big impact from minimal space.

So how do we densify our cities? From a parasitic hut in Ecuador to wafer-thin houses in Japan, from micro-apartments in Hong Kong to infill architecture in London, that's what this book endeavors to find out.

Chris Precht

An uncompromising approach to a demanding site

- PROMENADE HOUSE
- FORM / KOUICHI KIMURA ARCHITECTS
- SHIGA, JAPAN

Although the exterior is dramatic, this family home has an even more extraordinary interior, shaped by the extreme proportions of the site. The building is 9 feet (2.7 meters) wide and 89 feet (27 meters) long, filling the plot almost entirely. Inside, a series of rooms arranged along extended hallways heightens awareness of the long, thin space. "Your body senses the site geometry," the architect explains.

Within this uncompromising scheme, there is a surprising variety of room shapes and sizes, including two double-height volumes—a study and an enclosed balcony—that allow light to enter the concrete building shell. Other windows are deliberately small, creating privacy and a secluded feel. On the upper level, especially, there are playful touches: a curtain divides family rooms from the main passageway, and bright turquoise walls interrupt the monochrome scheme, creating what the architects call an "impression of cleanliness" in the family bathrooms.

Previous pages
An austere, slate gray, windowless facade greets visitors on arrival, and there are very few openings on the long sides of the house.

Current pages
Predominantly white, black, and gray in palette, spots of bold color add accents here and there. Examples include the bright yellow frames around the windows and green paneled walls in the hallway.

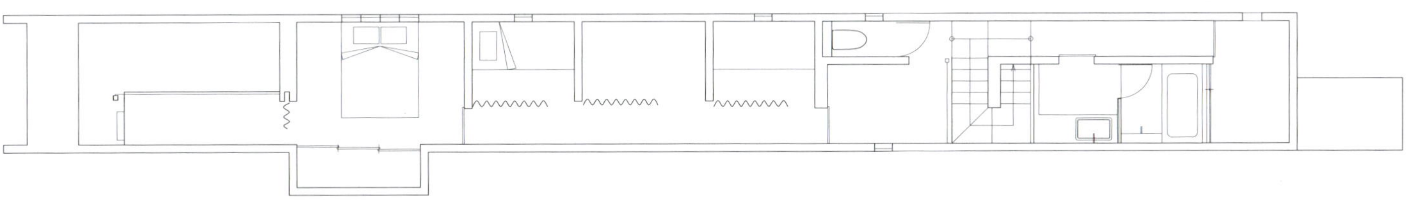

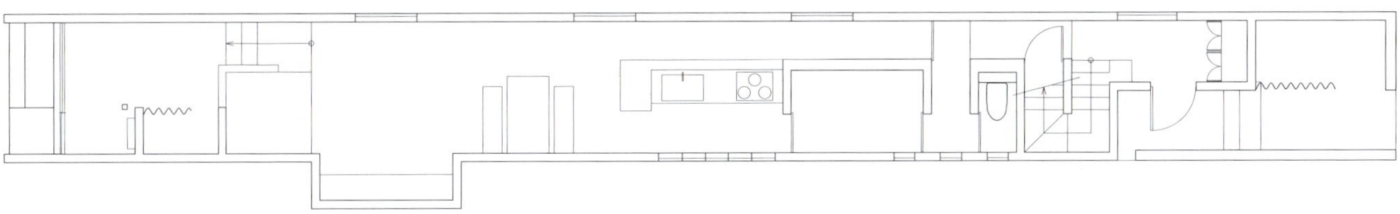

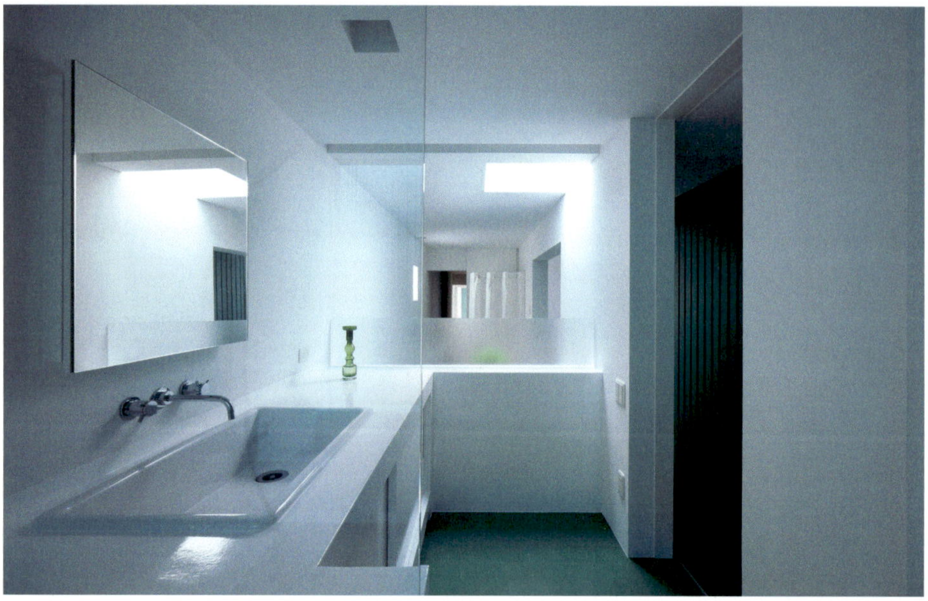

The house is three times as long as it is wide. Inside, the architects emphasize this length with long narrow corridors, with the living spaces unfolding as you venture farther.

Harmony prevails in this mixed-use, split-level structure

- CH HOUSE
- ODDO ARCHITECTS
- HANOI, VIETNAM

This slim, clean volume contrasts with, and towers above, its immediate neighbors. The simple facade is in counterpoint to the more haphazard appearance of nearby buildings and somewhat belies the complexity within. The long, thin, irregularly shaped plot was maximized to provide a two-story commercial space with a three-story multigenerational family home above it.

This combination of functions and priorities could have resulted in compromise, but the structure is both dramatic and elegant. The upper floors—home to family life—are characterized by fragmented floor plates, vast apertures, and full-height voids, which are planted with towering trees and plants. The rooms are surprisingly open and airy, illuminated by sunlight pouring in through the glass facade. Toward the rear of the building, the three main bedrooms, stacked one above the other, take advantage of the relative quiet in this part of the house.

ÁNH TUYẾT
SỰ KIỆN
CƯỚI HỎI
IN THIẾP CƯỚI
DỊCH VỤ HOA TƯƠI
ÁNH TUYẾT

Previous pages
A skin of perforated cement blocks allows natural light and ventilation to enter the house, while shielding the interior from dust and direct sunlight.

Current pages
Spaces are hard-working, keeping the house bright, multifunctional, and clutter free: folding screens offer options for privacy, open staircases make rooms airy, and clever storage solutions abound.

The incorporation of mature plants and trees helps to rebuild the link between humans and nature that is often lost in the urban environment.

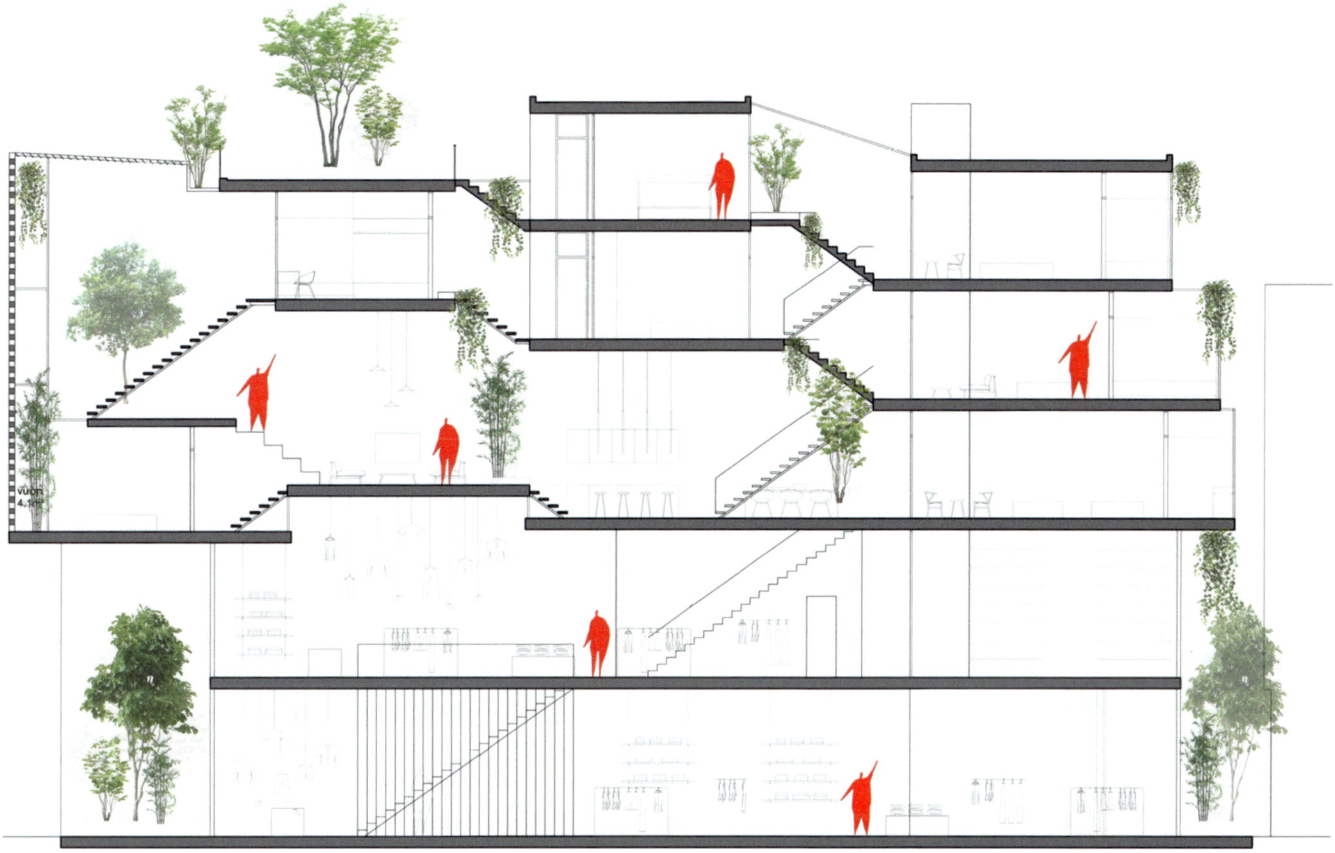

Constraints from within and without create a gently waving house

- NAMI-NAMI HOUSE
- YOSHINORI SAKANO ARCHITECTS
- TOKYO, JAPAN

The elderly owners of this house did not wish to relocate away from their familiar neighborhood, so their existing home—with steep stairs and narrow rooms—was demolished and completely rebuilt in this light and accessible form.

In addition to the need for flexible, accessible spaces inside, the architects faced site restrictions that reduced the already small plot to a buildable area of under 237 square feet (22 square meters). This distinctive "cut-out" volume is the result. Squeezing three stories into the space meant that room height was also limited, hence the barrel-vaulted ceilings, which maximize ceiling height while retaining space for hidden wiring and services. These design features, rather than appearing fussy, bring playfulness to an otherwise minimal home—the light that floods in through rear-facing windows bounces around, creating a gentle, comfortable feel.

Previous pages
This house is not much taller than its neighbors, but accommodates three stories to their two.

Current pages
A dominant feature in the house is the wave-like vaulting of the ceiling—a feature that helps to create an illusion of space.

A home of clarity and sensitivity

- TOWN HOUSE
- ELDING OSCARSON
- LANDSKRONA, SWEDEN

Like many of the other buildings featured in this book, Town House contends with the difficulties of a long, narrow plot in a crowded urban environment with limited access to light and space. The relative lack of partitions, the use of large window apertures, and broken-up floor plates are common to many such projects, but these bare facts do not communicate the unique character of this home, which combines minimalism with charm and thoughtful detail. The architect describes the dwelling as a "small-scale, motley, naturally worn place."

The long-term comfort of residents on this tiny (and previously long-empty) plot, in what is a fairly deprived region, depends on a sensitive and sustainable approach. The interior spaces are neither exposed nor confined, with the positioning of windows, skylights, and the interior courtyard bringing the outside in, while the key living areas are oriented in such a way that they remain private. Office space is provided in a separate outdoor volume, which simultaneously forms a boundary with a neighboring property.

Previous pages The house sits in a street of buildings that vary widely in height, size, facade material, age, and approach.

Current pages Thin, exposed steel slabs span the entire width of the house, dividing it horizontally and vertically, yet giving the impression of one continuous open space.

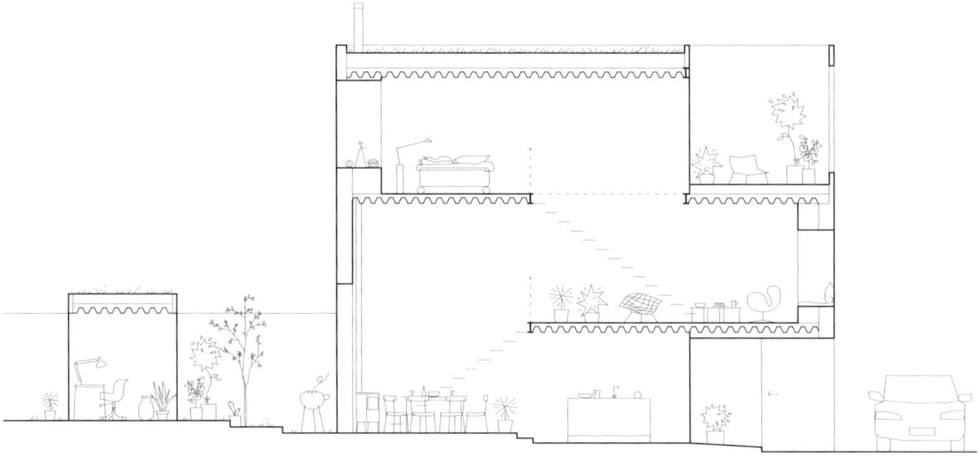

A compact courtyard space separates the main dwelling from the office space that flanks the boundary wall.

High drama and low-energy

- GAP HOUSE
- PITMAN TOZER ARCHITECTS
- LONDON, U.K.

A ground-floor corridor leads from the outrageously skinny frontage to the grand feature of this house: an open-plan living and dining area with a mezzanine, which spills out into a paved courtyard. Above, a series of tapering volumes—nested mostly in what was once a dark, narrow alley between the two neighboring buildings—houses bedrooms, bathrooms, and a third-floor conservatory. Such is the drama of the design that this house's eco-credentials could be overlooked.

Winner of the 2009 RIBA Manser Medal, Pitman Tozer's creation was recognized for creating "apparently generous spaces, despite all the constraints," but many of its most striking features are invisible. A ground-coupled heat pump served by three 164-foot-deep (50-meter-deep) boreholes provides all heating for the house, and extensive insulation—mostly naturally sourced and sustainable—keeps that heat inside. Rainwater is harvested to minimize consumption. Even the sculptural spiral staircase has a role to play, providing passive ventilation throughout the four-story structure in the warmer months.

The living room opens up onto the courtyard, a dramatic contrast to the slender facade.

ALMA-NAC

Over the past ten years, this London-based practice has grappled with some of the city's most confined spaces

Founded by architects Chris Bryant, Caspar Rodgers, and Tristan Wigfall, the London-based design and research practice set out an unconventional approach from the very beginning. When they first set up shop, the three directors drew attention for their guerrilla-style sidewalk set-ups with posters offering "FREE ARCHITECTURE" to passersby. By listening to London residents' understanding and requirements for architecture, they were able to kickstart several builds responding to specific needs.

"You can tell from the names of our designs that we like playing with the fact that they are infill projects."

London's soaring house prices and scarcity of space means most of its residents need to do more with less space. "The compact nature of the houses we build means that they are almost like large pieces of furniture," says Wigfall. "They have to fit around the inhabitants that live within them, so we draw inspiration from small structures, installations, and even sculptures." Making the most of restricted spaces or discovering the untapped potential in existing structures is an "enjoyable challenge" for alma-nac, which today comprises a collaborative team of eight. "You can tell from the names of our designs that we like playing with the fact that they are infill projects," Wigfall notes. Homes like Slim House, In-Betweeny House, and Wedge House have led alma-nac to venture into urban dentistry, a concept attributed to British Civic Architect John Thorp. "We thought the term was quite an apt description of our practice because we work with little nooks and crannies that are leftover—like the tiny spaces in between teeth."

Slim House

Alma-nac's first scheme tackling the challenge of constrained space was Slim House, which stands on the 7.5-foot-wide (2.3-meter-wide) site of a 19th-century stable between two historic properties on St John's Hill, a bustling street in Clapham Old Town, London. Their inventive extension of the pre-existing two-story home, completed in 2012, is characterized by a gently sloping slate roof punctured with generous oak-framed skylights that allow natural light to flood into each story, transforming the dark narrow interiors into surprisingly bright and spacious rooms.

In addition to the tiny lot, the architects also faced several other challenges, including the historic district's stringent planning restrictions, and the client's tight budget. "That's partly what drove the idea of the sloped roof," says Wigfall, who explains that "it is a very simple construction to work with, as the detailing is the same all the way down." The slate cladding blends in with the adjacent Victorian buildings. This meant that they could avoid changing the roofline, which would have been problematic for planning reasons. Additionally, by staggering the skylights, the architects were able "to play around with the scale of the spaces," says Wigfall. They extended the property at the back, adding a new dining area and an additional bedroom, as well as enlarging the master bedroom. Elevated ceilings on the two upper levels compensate for the limited headroom where the floors meet the slope of the roof. On the ground floor, the welcoming entrance reveals a view through the sunlit dining area to the kitchen and the garden outside. →

Slim House
The architects raked the roof and dotted it with skylights so that light could enter each floor of the building, which has no windows on its outer walls.

In-Betweeny House
A narrow, two-story annex to an existing four-story building enables the original building to function as two houses, one sandwiched between the other.

In-Betweeny House

This micro extension, completed in 2017, forms a self-contained two-story home nestled alongside—and connected to—a house in Lambeth, South London. Working with a plot only 5.2 feet (1.6 meters) wide, architect Caspar Rodgers explains that "their brief was to utilize the unused space beside the main house to improve the living arrangements for a young family." He also explains that "the original house had a large yet under-used ground floor, and a smaller, dark, but much-used lower ground floor." By adding several new spaces and adapting the adjoining areas in the original house, they reorganized the internal flow and eased the transition between the two dwellings. Working in collaboration with their clients, alma-nac maximized the flexibility of the extension by enabling the family to open up or close off the new spaces with a set of folding doors, and the separate front door allows the extension to function completely independently, as required.

Sizeable skylights in the new bathroom and kitchen, as well as two extra openings on the original facade, form the naturally bright interior. The geometric "goose-eye" tiles that cover the exterior walls next to the front door are also used in the living spaces, creating a characterful feel that contrasts with the yellow brick used to blend the extension with the main house and the neighboring properties. Elements from the original home were also repurposed in the extension. For example, copper roofing panels form kitchen and bathroom counters.

Wedge House

Another of alma-nac's ingenious infill projects is the two-story Wedge House in Southwark, southeast London. The dwelling, built in 2018, is squeezed between two traditional Victorian terraces, on a tapered slice of land that once housed a car garage. "Convincing the city planners of the quality of space that we intended to create in such a confined space was quite a challenge," Wigfall recalls. "Effectively, the site has a footprint equivalent to a one-bedroom flat, but we built a three-story house." The studio worked with the client to devise the program, designing it from the inside out. They prioritized living space and functional storage, creating an open-plan layout with minimal circulation space. Skylights and large windows overlook the garden at the rear, drawing in natural light and enhancing the overall impression of spaciousness. The interiors have a simple stripped-back aesthetic—the softwood timber frame is exposed and untreated, as is the open-tread staircase.

In addition to infill houses, alma-nac brings their knowledge and experience of working with restricted plots to find new ways of densifying existing sites. Their work has attracted the attention of housing developers who have approached them with questions such as: "Can we densify our sites by using some of the principles you've developed through your infill housing?" or "I've got this tiny sliver of land, can I squeeze a house into it?" By way of research, teaching, and an exhaustive iterative process, alma-nac considers the user experience above all else. Although they've taken down the "FREE ARCHITECTURE" sign, they maintain an in-depth dialogue with their clients from the beginning to the end of their projects. ●

Wedge House
This house in particular reflects alma-nac's interest in what they call "urban dentistry:" the densification of urban environments, through

Inspired by the Victorian coach house

- THE COACH HOUSE
- SELENCKY /// PARSONS
- LONDON, U.K.

The bold facade of this family home is inspired by the pillars of the coach house that once stood on this site, with some of the brickwork reclaimed from the original structure. Jutting concrete-coated slabs are juxtaposed with the three-level Victorian buildings on either side, making this a striking addition to a conventional residential street.

The appeal of the house is such that it was even featured by the *British Press* website when it went up for sale in January 2020—perhaps unsurprising, given its elegant, minimal aesthetic. The main volume—a three-story, 11.5-foot-wide (3.5-meter-wide) unit, on the site of the former building—makes a virtue of its extreme height, with a central staircase that is dominated by a dramatic light fixture hanging down through all three stories. The first floor, which wraps around the back of the neighboring house, is also inventive: a sunken living space means that, despite being open plan, the family area is separate and snug. This is something quite different from the ubiquitous London terrace extension.

What starts as a narrow house overlooking the street expands to more than twice in width toward the back, where the principal family rooms—kitchen, living room, and dining room—inhabit generous spaces overlooking the garden.

Inventive design in tight quarters

- EAST HARLEM HOUSING
- ROBERT MARINO ARCHITECTS
- NEW YORK CITY, USA

At just over 18 feet (5.5 meters) wide, this is a slender home in a populous city. The limited plot and the need to comply with New York's housing regulations on bedroom width meant that cantilevers were required to create enough space for two-bedroom units on three of the levels. The bedrooms are situated at the back of the building and each has a window overlooking the back garden. Meanwhile, the kitchen-dining-living rooms in each unit look out over the street, and storage and services are clustered around the central stairwell.

A one-bedroom penthouse occupies the top story, while the first two floors contain the only unit with a staircase, which has three bedrooms. A variety of forms and uses have been achieved within the building, but they are unified by the inventive street-facing facade with irregular, chamfered window openings that give the building character and a degree of separation from the street.

Essential innovations for a familiar residential format

- BARRETTS GROVE
- GROUPWORK
- LONDON, U.K.

This six-unit housing block has a great deal packed behind a relatively narrow facade: a one-bedroom apartment on the ground floor, three two-bed units, and two three-bed units, including a penthouse. The interiors are spacious, bright, and contemporary, with an emphasis on warm-toned timber, but its most striking contribution to this typology is not immediately apparent: innovative design and building processes have reduced the carbon footprint and building costs of the project substantially.

The building as a whole takes a formidable, symmetrical form. Cross-laminated timber (CLT) has been used structurally in combination with the red brick that is so characteristic of suburban London to form a "skin" that wraps around the entire building. Inside, the CLT is left visible, is varnished, and paired with a restricted palette of finishings (such as rubber flooring to waterproof bathrooms). This decision, along with a careful, holistic design strategy and close collaboration between the architects, contractors, and client, demonstrates what is possible in a multi-dwelling block.

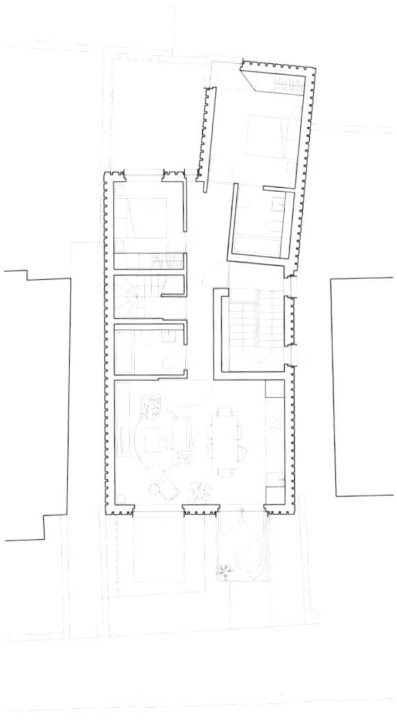

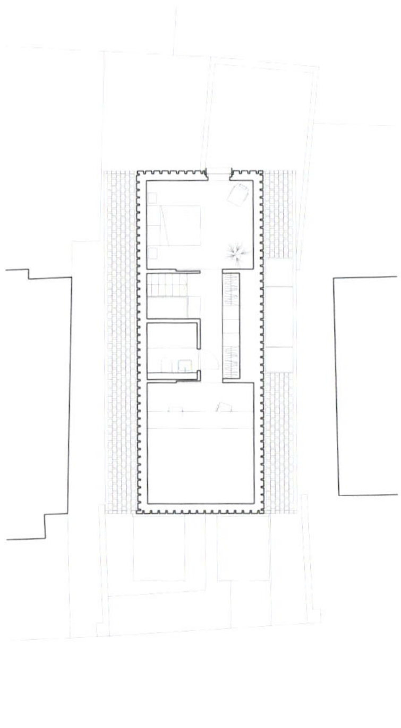

Previous pages
The red-brick facade is a decorative skin, rather than a supporting structure.

Current pages
Oversized steel balconies protrude from the facade, alternating with large windows; the balconies are woven with wicker to soften their effect.

The exposed timber structure creates a warm, tactile interior, contrasted with exposed brick elements throughout.

COMPACT LIVING COMMUNITIES

Shared housing has rapidly gained popularity due to lifestyle changes and the rising cost of living, but only time will tell whether it is a viable long-term solution or just a passing trend.

In the past ten years, the term co-living has taken on a new, broader definition that goes hand in hand with sustainability, affordability, and environmental and social impact. Co-living developments like Common in New York, and the Collective in London, carved a new path for community-based living where residents are not merely tenants, but "members." The concept is certainly not new, but as more people move to urban environments with an inadequate supply of affordable housing, micro-apartment and tiny pod communities offer a practical, low-cost solution for transitional residents seeking an antidote to the loneliness and isolation of city living.

During the early 20th century, waves of immigrants arrived in industrialized cities, including London, New York, and Chicago, and flexible hotel room rentals or SROs (single room occupancy housing) became a popular form of accommodation for people of all income levels working in busy downtown areas. But as the housing market picked up and the wealthy moved to the suburbs in the late 1950s, they became pejoratively known as flophouses or cage hotels, and they were eventually bought out or made illegal, putting entire communities out on the streets.

In Hong Kong, where land is owned by the government and leased or sold to developers at auction, affordable housing has been reduced to cage- or coffin-like spaces that can barely fit two people at a time, with poor ventilation, no natural light, and kitchens and bathrooms shared by four to six families. A similar style of communal accommodation emerged in the Soviet Union during the early 20th century in response to a housing crisis. Known as *Kommunalki,* the apartments offered residents single rooms, which served as living, dining, and bedrooms for whole families, and communal kitchens, bathrooms, and corridors shared by up to seven families.

[1]

[2]

"It's a fine balance between the quality of the design and healthy living environments."

In other words, this model has been tried before, and it's no surprise that it is being "re-invented" given that the densification of cities is increasing. However, the newly popular co-living lifestyle invites people to live in "micro-lofts," pods, or capsules, with the promise of building a community with the comfort and convenience of "serviced living." Some architects, working closely with the communities they serve, believe there is much more to it. Architect Tristan Wigfall of London-based practice alma-nac understands the idea of co-living is still in its infancy and is likely not meant for everyone: "We're going through the experimentation phase at the moment," Wigfall notes. "It's a fine balance between ensuring the quality of the design in order to create sustainable and healthy living environments." Alma-nac's Paxton House—which was informed by their 7.5-foot-wide (2.3-meter-wide) Slim House—is a co-living project comprised of 43 "micro-units" that share a workspace, roof garden, and a spare bedroom that can be booked for friends and family as needed. "Where you create compact living environments," Wigfall says, "you need to make sure that there are additional amenities, so that while residents might be limited in living space, there are further opportunities within the wider building and city beyond it." →

[3]

MODULAR CO-HOUSING

Careful design solutions that veer away from the usual container or capsule models and focus on the occupant's well-being can create welcoming, healthier city-living alternatives.

In Seoul, which has a population of over nine million people, the architecture firm SsD led by Jinhee Park, developed the microhousing building Songpa, which offers shared amenities and a combination of private and public space, creating a flexible community where residents can live and work. Park explains that the "units can be adapted for differing programs, such as galleries or workspaces, allowing occupants to live in the building for longer because they won't need to move out as their situation changes." The 14 units are equipped with Murphy beds and micro-kitchens with two-burner induction stoves and pull-out counter space. Clerestory windows provide natural light and create the impression of higher ceilings without reducing wall space or compromising residents' privacy. There is a shared auditorium-cum-living room, sunken courtyards, and light wells that make the communal areas pleasant spaces for the residents to spend time in. The entire building is enveloped in a screen of slightly twisted metal strips that protect, shade, and even help canalize rainwater down the facade.

Unfortunately, modular housing can get as constrictive as the 107-square-foot (10-square-meter) units in São Paulo's VN Nova Higienópolis. The developer argues that the micro-apartments are primarily for sleeping or resting, while the rest of the building includes generous shared spaces. Some might compare these types of spatial restraints to prison-like conditions, but others contend that it is a viable solution, which could help to address the global housing crisis. However, quarantine measures during the COVID-19 pandemic have arguably made this type of accommodation unviable.

COHABITATION COMMUNITIES

The benefits of keeping a certain level of privacy while sharing some amenities can give residents a feeling of ownership and freedom and reduce a community's carbon footprint without compromising on the quality of life.

Before the global housing crisis hit, buying a house or an apartment was a generational marker for the start of adulthood. However, as homeownership becomes increasingly unattainable, the alternative of a more flexible, mobile lifestyle is more desirable and seemingly unavoidable. In Barcelona, Miel Arquitectos, in collaboration with designers Studio P10, have explored what they call "flexible coexistence," which they believe is the future of a lifestyle that will become increasingly nomadic. Their 2014 project, Salva46, is a 700-square-foot (65-square-meter) refurbished apartment with a central kitchen and living space, and two micro-studio apartments on either side, each with a bed, bath, and mezzanine space that can be blocked off with sliding doors. And while this setup might sound like a new version of "living with roommates," their adaptive reuse project is more of an experiment in viable cohabiting without the loss of privacy. The configuration can also be transformed to accommodate a family.

The question of whether or not the sharing system works and whether it can alleviate the global housing crisis is still up for debate, and

[4]

[5]

[5]

sometimes aspirational marketing strategies like The Collective's invitation to "join the global living movement" play a large role in coaxing people into microliving communities. Language is crucial and can often be deceptive. A similar effect is the concept of the starter home, which in reality ends up being a substandard version of the "ideal" home one wishes to acquire.

Constellation ATX, an estate of 83 micro-homes in an area of 6.2 acres (2.5 hectares) south of Austin, Texas, offers the promise of joining a community. Modules that offer both private and community living are provided by U.S.-based companies, such as Sprout Tiny Homes and Kasita, which produces stackable units. Likewise, LuxTiny in Arizona provides custom designs for first-time homeowners or retired couples wishing to downsize. However, the tiny eclectic-styled homes have poor circulation solutions, and they are surrounded by sparse landscape that does not seem particularly conducive to creating a community or offering access to shared outdoor space. Unsurprisingly, the backlash faced by these types of developments, which have been dubbed "gentrified trailer parks," has caused enough of a controversy to stall their construction, at least in the case of Constellation ATX.

> "These types of developments, which have been dubbed 'gentrified trailer parks,' have caused enough of a controversy to stall their construction."

It will take time to determine whether micro-living communities will become a new way of life or a fleeting trend, but as long as the cost of living continues to rise, due either to land scarcity or poor land management, the sharing economy is likely to impact all areas of our lives, including our homes. However, in an era when physical distancing measures quickly became the new norm, sharing and cohabiting are destined to become increasingly fraught. ●

[1] ISA's Sheridan Street Housing project, Philadelphia.

[2] LOT-EK's modular Drivelines Studios in Johannesburg, South Africa, is made of 140 upcycled shipping containers.

[3] The inner courtyard of LOT-EK's Drivelines Studios, where staircases and bridges connect the two buildings.

[4] One of the bedrooms inside Miel's Salva46 in Barcelona.

[5] Treehouse by architecture studio Bo.Daa sets a new trend for youth housing in Seoul, South Korea.

A new lease on life for Rotterdam's iconic warehouse

- FENIX I
- MEI ARCHITECTS AND PLANNERS
- ROTTERDAM, NETHERLANDS

In this merging of old and new, Rotterdam's monumental 1920s Fenix warehouse—once one of the world's largest—now serves as the supporting structure of a sizeable mixed-use development. The warehouse itself contains quay houses, offices, a bed-and-breakfast, and an extensive culture cluster; the century-old building has become a thriving hotspot in its own right. Up above are up to nine stories of loft apartments—more than 200 of them—in a range of sizes, many with stunning views over the harbor. Somewhat rare in loft-style complexes of this scale, the developers were hugely flexible in their approach, allowing buyers to determine the size and layout of their apartments, and even whether to arrange them over one floor or two. In keeping with the developer's request to preserve the industrial character of the warehouse and its history, the lofts are raised up on an enormous space-frame structure that stands on the roof of the original warehouse, marking the transition from last century to the current one.

Previous pages
In keeping with the surrounding buildings, Fenix I has nine stories on the Rijnhaven side but is limited to four stories on the Veerlaan side.

Current pages
The mixed-use areas of the development include a gym in the warehouse building (below). It has become a true community building, both for residents and the neighborhood as a whole.

A farm in the middle of the city

● THE FARMHOUSE
● PRECHT

In this design for high-rise modular homes, Precht have gone beyond the need simply to alleviate housing shortages. They have also introduced a vertical farming system that, if the concept were adopted in cities across the globe, could help to slow climate change and alleviate food shortages. Essentially, a series of timber frames is attached to the facade of the building, alternating with outdoor terraces, and designed in such a way that homeowners can grow their own food. Not only does the concept reacquaint urbanites with agriculture, but growing locally also shortens supply chains and reduces the use of packaging. Added to these admirable attempts at sustainable living, the concept also has systems in place for reusing the building's heat to help grow plants, to recycle rainwater, and to make compost for the gardens from food waste. The potential for a circular community model, where residents share or trade food, electricity, and gardening-related facilities, is an attractive prospect for urban developments of the future.

Previous pages
Each timber module is made of three layers: utility, insulation and the garden elements.

Current pages
Developments such as this would introduce some much-needed greenery into the world's densest urban centers.

Inhabitants would be offered the chance to personalize their space, choosing from a range of options for kitchens and bedrooms, balconies, and gardens.

This page
Being in such close proximity to healthy plants, and nurturing them from seed to harvest reconnects city-dwellers with nature on a personal level.

Opposite
The garden frames are designed in such a way that several homes can share the upkeep of one large space or opt to tend just their own garden.

Passer Domesticus

Unvarnished comfort in an unusual rental home

- PASSER DOMESTICUS
- 157+173 DESIGNERS
- THESSALONIKI, GREECE

Unfinished surfaces, reclaimed furniture, and a charming yet diverse material palette: this is space-efficient urban living without the high shine. This tiny holiday rental is the brainchild of architect duo Babis Papanikolaou and Christina Tsirangelou, who created the home for city-break visitors interested in a more unique, street-level experience in the ancient Greek port city.

Formerly a textiles shop, then a fishing accessories store, this 1924 building belongs to the simple, two-story typology widely built in Thessaloniki after its great fire of 1917, with Byzantine and neoclassical architecture references. Rich in history and short on floor space—each level measures 172 square feet (16 square meters)—it has been updated to take advantage of dead zones, such as the "mezzanine" level created above the first floor using a fisherman's net, while retaining its overall form. Finishing is key throughout, from the white-painted original wooden floor on the upper level through to the brick and pink marble used in the basement shower area, a reference to the famous Bezesteni Ottoman market that stands nearby.

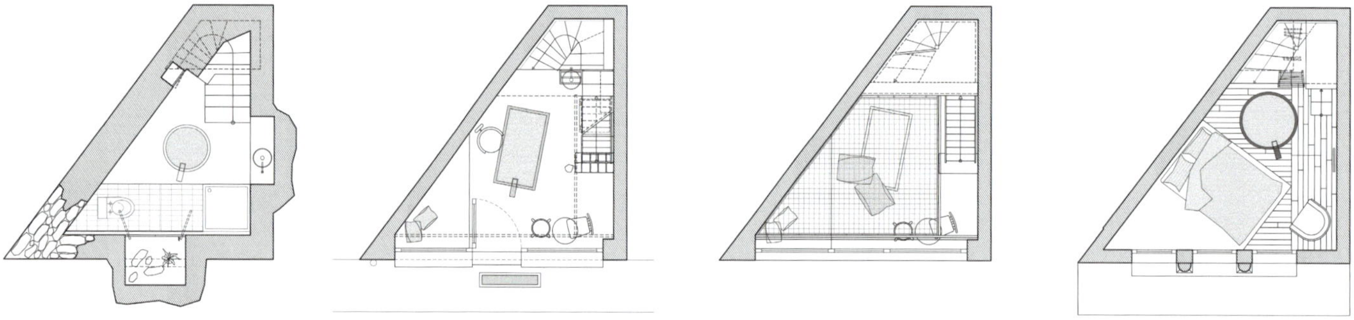

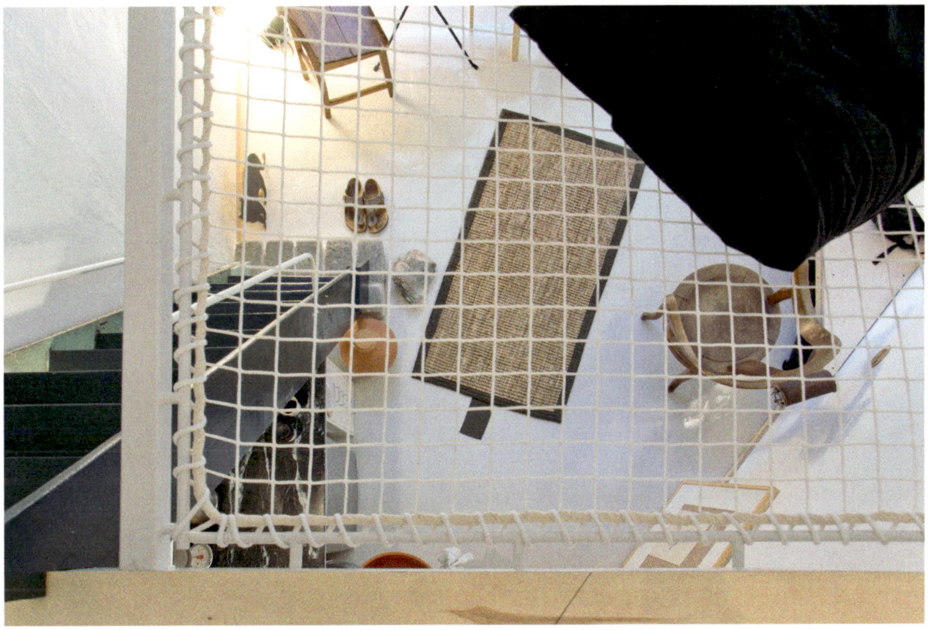

The architects have found innovative ways to adapt what is, in effect, a very small triangular space to suit the purpose of each room.

A Dickensian nook, reimagined

- ARCHWAY STUDIOS
- UNDERCURRENT ARCHITECTS
- LONDON, U.K.

Victorian rail viaducts slice through South London, with the arches and surroundings often used for light industry. The outer cladding of this live-work space reflects that context. Inside, however, everything is clean and serene. A slim four-story atrium has been grafted to the outside of the viaduct, with light pouring in through a skylight, the glass facade, and slits in the building's steel skin. Inside the arch itself, meanwhile, the living area opens up, with light conceived by the architects as an "excavating force," focused by the concave outer wall of the atrium and burrowing into the interior.

The building exists in the context of an effort to solve problems associated with London's complex infrastructure, with the local council relaxing planning rules in an attempt to open up spaces like rail arches and prevent them from dividing local communities. Such sites require thoughtful planning and construction; here, for example, stressed-skin construction from aircraft manufacturing was employed to create a thin, robust building shell and maximize the space available.

Previous pages
The narrow site is cocooned within a slender steel shell, which offers acoustic protection from the inner-city sounds, among them the trains passing close by.

Current pages
Light penetrates even the deepest reaches of the interior thanks to a long skylight at the top and the rear wall, made entirely of glass.

The vast, geometric proportions of the railway arch contrast against the sinuous, sculptural forms of the three-story annex.

SIM-PLEX DESIGN STUDIO

In an ultradense vertical city like Hong Kong, this local practice makes a small amount of space go a long way.

Architect Patrick Lam spent the first 30 years of his life living in a tenement apartment in Kowloon Walled City, north of Hong Kong. Kowloon was originally a Chinese military fort, which remained autonomously governed through the Opium Wars with Britain in the 19th century. In the 1940s, the high-density enclave was reclaimed by Hong Kong, but it was never fully incorporated under their rule, leading to severe problems with drug crime and squatters. By 1990, Kowloon had a population of 50,000 people living in just 5 acres (20,000 square meters), but it retained elements of a village because the buildings were interconnected. "I had to climb five flights of stairs to get home," says Lam, "but passing the neighbors each day helped us to get to know one another and created a strong sense of community."

Growing up in Kowloon, his family of four maximized their home by using space-saving solutions such as bunk beds and folding doors, a personal experience that has influenced his work as an architect. After studying in Hong Kong, he went on to found Sim-Plex Design Studio, which has tackled residential projects in some of the most confined apartments in Hong Kong. Lam is passionate about "enhancing limited spaces without compromising living standards for residents," and Sim-Plex's projects focus on innovative solutions that maximize the space available.

Adaptable Architecture

A project that embodies Sim-Plex's design approach is Pets Playground, a 453-square-foot (42-square-meter) apartment in Yuen Long, Hong Kong, for a young couple with a pet parrot, as well as an elderly parent and her cat. "The pets are considered members of the family, with personalities of their own, and they needed separate spaces," Lam explains. Multifunctionality and flexibility are paramount in a limited space, especially when different generations are living under the same roof. Lam's versatile scheme for the apartment includes space-efficient fixtures and fittings, including three sliding fritted glass doors that allow the family to adapt the living areas to form communal and private areas as needed, without blocking the light. The elevated seating platform doubles as a storage box, and the dining table and chairs can be tucked away when they are not in use. Platforms and cubby holes for the cat to explore are integrated into the cabinets and wardrobes, which are made from environmentally friendly melamine-faced boards to protect them from the cat's claws.

Understanding the clients' priorities, routines, and how they use their home is a critical component of Sim-Plex's design process. For Pretty House in Pink, Sim-Plex was asked to design an apartment for a young woman to suit her lifestyle and reflect her personality. The 1986 movie *Pretty in Pink* served as a reference for female empowerment (the film touches upon class differences and high-school prom drama). The combination of gold accents and detailing on the furniture and pink-painted window frames was inspired by the lead character's costumes. The effect is a warm feminine feel with a subtle nod to the 1980s, without overplaying the theme. The apartment's most striking feature is the dressing table with a semicircular mirror and light bulbs in the walk-in closet area. The walls are painted in muted pastel gray and pink tones, evoking a feeling of calm. →

Smart Zendo

This 527-square-foot (49-square-meter) apartment manages to combine an impressive smart technology system within surroundings that respect the rules of feng-shui for achieving natural harmony in the home.

Bay House (this page)
Pretty House in Pink (opposite)

Both exemplify the studio's skill at carrying a concept through all aspects of their design, from spatial arrangements and materials to furnishings and color schemes.

For the Bay House, a young couple approached Lam with the task of renovating their 495-square-foot (46-square-meter) apartment with three vast bay windows overlooking outstanding views of the bay. "They asked for a flexible arrangement of the space without obstructing views of the scenery outside." Lam treated the windows as "multifunctional picture frames." Storage cabinets, shelves, and light fittings are integrated with the deep wooden window frames, and the sills can be used for a variety of different purposes, reducing the need for additional furniture. In the main living space, for instance, the dining table rolls out from a wall, and the window sill provides seating in the place of dining chairs. The other two windows are in the master bedroom and home-office space, offering beautiful views and plentiful natural light. "Oversized bay windows were very popular in Hong Kong in the early 2000s," says Lam, explaining that "due to a quirk in building regulations, windowsills were exempt from floor space restrictions, which prompted developers to build properties with increasingly deep bay windows." This is no longer the case, but, as Bay House proves, they can be utilized to increase the functionality of small spaces.

"Windowsills were exempt from floor space restrictions, which prompted developers to build increasingly deep bay windows."

The Smart Home

Smart homes quickly became popular in Hong Kong, but Lam laments that smart technology is not always integrated in a harmonious way. "Although feng shui aesthetics and smart technology seem to be contradictory," Lam notes, Smart Zendo shows how they can be entirely compatible—"if applied properly." The renovation project was commissioned by a young couple with a deep affinity for the principles of traditional Chinese living. The modest apartment is also home to the couple's child and occasionally his grandmother, so it was crucial for the scheme to be versatile. A combination of cutting-edge technology and traditional feng shui principles allows the apartment to adapt to their busy lifestyle with time-saving functions that are built in, such as voice-activated lighting systems and automated air-conditioning, curtain opening, projection screens, and electronic door locks. Bespoke maple wood paneling conceals the workings of the tech, creating a sleek, minimal aesthetic, while the layout and positioning of the furniture adhere to feng shui principles of balance and harmony. The living room has been raised to accommodate storage boxes underneath, as well as a table that lifts up when it is needed. Sliding doors can be closed to separate the kitchen area, and it can comfortably accommodate a variety of activities, from tea ceremonies to movie nights, as well as space for the couple's son to play. Smart Zendo is an artful combination of old and new, a fitting distinction considering the feng shui principles that defined the space. As Lam explains, "The spirit of Zen is the pursuit of harmony." ●

Pets Playground

Even with the most unusual briefs, Sim-Plex rises to the challenge of accommodating a diverse range of inhabitants in confined spaces, so that all have a degree of freedom and comfort.

Microliving in a former taxicab office

- 13 M^2 HOUSE
- STUDIOMAMA
- LONDON, U.K.

A quintessentially modern statement, with its candy-colored fittings and birch ply construction, this innovative living space—a renovation of a former taxicab office—also has a touch of camp. From the fold-down bed, with a mirrored underside, to the diner-style seating, the interior is reminiscent of a mobile home, which was one of the models that multidisciplinary design duo Studiomama looked at when investigating space-saving solutions.

The awkward shape of the pre-existing plot here necessitated an original approach. Counters and constructions jut into the living area from all sides; the designers conceived a "series of volumetric spaces"—essentially five bespoke furniture units—that slot together to create one main room accommodating all the functions of day-to-day living. The emphasis is on dual-purpose structures with maximum built-in storage, including cabinets and shelves designed for specific items.

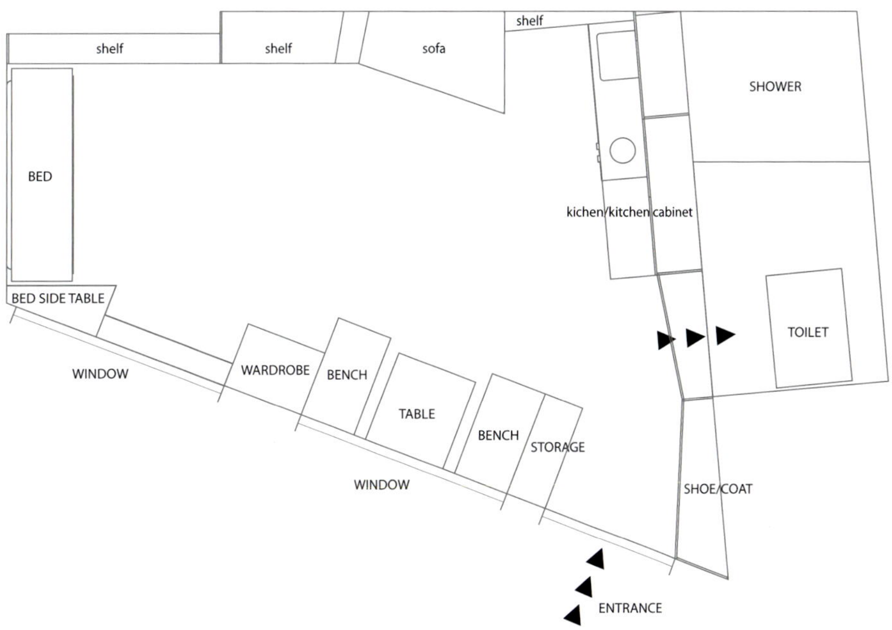

Previous page
The unassuming former taxicab office is seen from the outside. From the inside, the image shows the extendable dining setup.

This page
Most of the furnishings in this apartment can be tucked away when not in use. The Murphy bed folds up to reveal a small workspace and sitting area.

Much by little

- 17.6-SQUARE-METER APARTMENT
- A LITTLE DESIGN
- TAIPEI, TAIWAN

Having remodeled a similar apartment to much acclaim, Taiwanese practice A Little Design faced even more significant challenges in converting this tiny former piano teacher's studio into a functioning living space. Negotiating problems such as an almost 1.5-foot (50 centimeter) step in floor level, and an enormous concrete beam cutting across the ceiling, the designers transformed the meager apartment, creating new possibilities for this micro-apartment type of dwelling, common in Taipei City.

In addition to the usual small-space solutions of hidden storage and a limited material palette, the designers made more sweeping structural changes here—the bedroom mezzanine being the most obvious. With this new "room" in place, the apartment becomes a two-bed dwelling, with the daybed on the lower level available to accommodate guests. The bathroom is also ingenious, with huge mirrors and smart fittings that create a sense of luxury in a constrained space.

Previous pages
The ground floor living room is packed with neat solutions for making the space extra-efficient: a lift-up desktop/dining table; a built-in sofa; underfloor storage—every last space has its purpose.

Current pages
Cupboards line the stairs that rise up to the mezzanine sleeping area—the stairs themselves make access to the cupboards possible without a step ladder.

Undercounter shelving and high-level storage offer maximum space for crockery, utensils, and appliances in the kitchen. In the bathroom the sliding door is partially mirrored to make the room brighter and more spacious, visually.

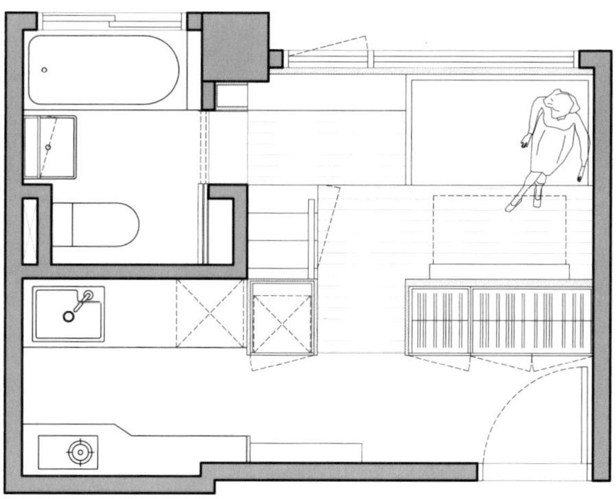

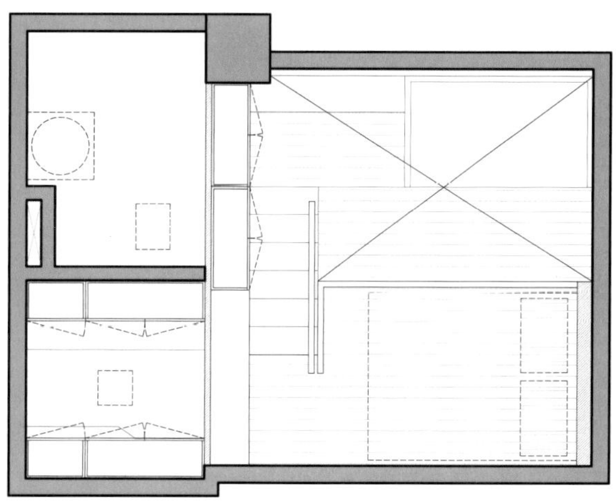

FLEXIBLE INTERIORS

Dynamic, adaptable interiors that can be tailored to residents' changing needs offer a glimpse of the future.

FOLDABLE, EXTENDABLE, MODULAR

Flexibility is crucial to the success of small homes because they must perform multiple functions, from home-working to entertaining, within a limited footprint. The rising cost of living in contemporary urban environments has meant that living space is increasingly limited, but many space reconfiguration concepts have been tried and tested over the years.

After the Second World War, a wide-spread housing crisis prompted leading European architects to develop adaptable and multipurpose architecture. They drew inspiration from compact accommodation, such as sleeper train carriages and ship's cabins, which Swiss architect Le Corbusier considered models for high-density housing. Modernism profoundly impacted many aspects of residential design, and the movement's groundbreaking approach to the function of buildings and the use of materials was responsible for the development of a new, more dynamic way of living.

Iconic early examples include Gerrit Rietveld's Schröderhuis (1924), which features sliding panels that allow the open-plan layout to be subdivided, and Pierre Chareau's Maison de Verre (1928–32), which incorporates innovations like mechanical louvered windows, Pirelli rubber flooring, and mobile metal screens. Among Le Corbusier's inventive concepts was Maison Loucheur (1928–29), a prefabricated *maison à sec,* or dry house, that could be assembled in a factory and then easily transported and reconfigured in single or multiple modules of 452 square feet (42 square meters). Industrial methods and materials, as well as mechanical solutions were integrated into design concepts at the outset, enabling spaces to be adapted by users and increasing the efficiency of domestic tasks.

[1]

[2]

"It's clear that resident participation is one of the most important elements in the success of these schemes."

While some architects, such as Bruno Taut, suggested that these solutions "could be applied to mass-housing" in reality, they were more suitable "for the one-off house with the modernist architect determining or, rather, over-determining the way spaces are used." However, it is clear that resident participation is one of the most, if not the most, important elements in the success of these types of schemes.

ADAPTABLE FURNITURE

Today, sliding screens, pull-out sofas, Murphy beds, moveable furniture, hidden storage, and concealed appliances are go-to solutions that enable residents to utilize every inch of their homes and reconfigure them for different purposes according to the time of day. Architect Nicholas Gurney employed many of these space-saving tools in a 258-square-foot (24-square-meter) micro-apartment in Sydney. The apartment is designed →

to adhere to the Japanese organizational method known as 5S—sort, set in order, standardize, sustain, and shine—in order to encourage a disciplined and efficient use of space. The open-plan layout has custom-built overhead storage, recessed lighting, and practical solutions, such as a perforated metal screen that rotates 180 degrees, allowing the television to be used in the living space and bedroom, and a rollout table with stackable Artek stools that can be tucked away when not in use, making space for other activities.

In countries with tropical climates, hammocks or suspended netting are often used to save space. Traditional-style Mayan homes are still built with an open oval-shaped plan with hammocks that allow the living space to double as a sleeping area at night. Similarly, in Rotterdam, architects Gwendolyn Huisman and Marijn Boterman's home SkinnySCAR includes a suspended net on the second floor alongside a double-height window, which allows them to utilize the space without restricting the light.

[4]

"An entire branch of the design industry emerged to take on the challenge of providing design solutions for small spaces."

With space at a premium, an entire branch of the design industry has emerged with an intent to take on the challenge of providing design solutions for small spaces. Clei in Italy and Resource Furniture in the United States, for instance, provide wall beds, expandable tables, sofas that turn into bunk beds, and home office and storage modules with different configurations. Ori Living, a spin-off of MIT Media Lab's CityHome project, is a lifestyle brand and product design company that takes this a step further with robotic furniture. Their designs include a bedroom that automatically transforms into a home office, as well as a space-saving walk-in closet that contracts into a desk and bookcase at the push of a button.

Tiny Home Bed, designed by Seoul-based designer Yesul Jang, is another excellent example of a product designed to make small spaces more livable. It provides additional storage space under the bed without compromising on aesthetics or taking up valuable floor space. Similarly, nmstudio's plywood pegboard modules for the Senri Yamada Nishi housing complex in Osaka offer versatile surfaces for displaying or storing personal effects, allowing residents to personalize their homes.

[3]

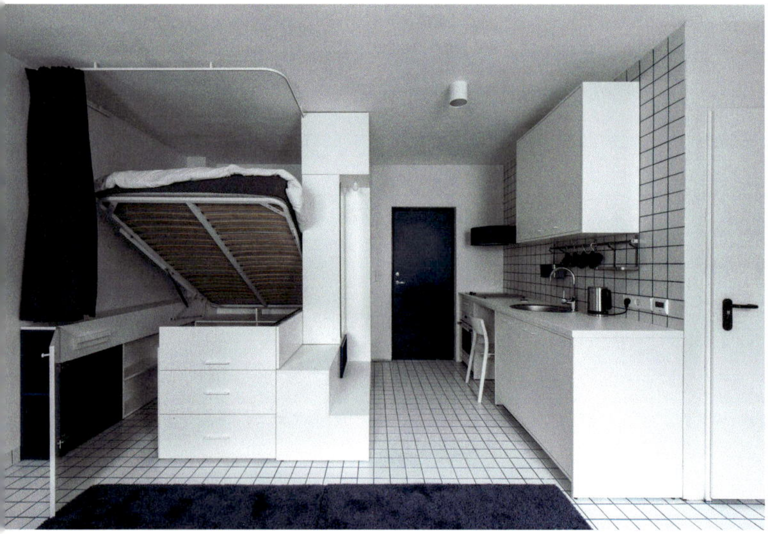

UTILITARIAN SURFACES

One of the most mundane and yet time-consuming aspects of keeping a practical home is cleaning. When Formica, the industrial melamine laminate par excellence, was introduced in the 1930s, it revolutionized countertops the world over because of its heat resistance, durability, and wipe-clean utility. Materials like stainless steel, sealed reinforced concrete, and ceramic tiles are similarly hard-wearing and low maintenance, making them

[5]

[5]

pragmatic choices for functional spaces like kitchens and bathrooms, and the fuss-free, unembellished aesthetic helps to create a more spacious feel.

Lebanese architect Elie Metni's design for a 172-square-foot (16-square-meter) micro-apartment named Shoebox exemplifies this approach. Perched on the roof of a building in the center of the Achrafieh district of Beirut, it has easy-to-clean surfaces like laminated plywood and bright white tiles that continue seamlessly from the bathroom to the kitchen on both walls and floor, enhancing the apartment's bright and airy feel and making cleaning a breeze.

Lithuania-based HEIMA architects also used white ceramic tiles to line four micro-apartments in Vilnius, but, in this case, they employed an unusual twist. In each flat, they used a different-colored grout to add warmth, unifying each space and differentiating it from the others without compromising the efficiency of cleaning the properties.

INTELLIGENT HOMES

Smart technology is another significant factor contributing to the flexibility of contemporary homes and can be used to ease small living. Our lives have been streamlined with smart appliances and voice-activated systems at a pace that was unimaginable just 10 years ago. Existing or newly built dwellings can now include a wide range of tools for programming the home, from portable speakers to home security and climate control, maximizing efficiency without reducing the available living space, and this promises to be an area of further development in the future.

Smart Zendo, a recent project by the Hong Kong-based design studio Sim-Plex, seamlessly integrates intelligent appliances with translucent partitions, built-in storage, and climate-control solutions that enhance the residents' quality of life. The concept "is based on the principles of Zen Buddhism with the aim of combining natural scenery, traditional feng shui aesthetics, and smart technology," explains architect Patrick Lam. The two-bedroom apartment includes a three-part fritted glass sliding partition that can be stowed away inside a wall when not needed. A raised wooden platform provides additional storage space without restricting the living space and also hides "an intelligent coffee table" that pops up when in use.

As the world changes at an ever-increasing pace and residential needs evolve accordingly, accommodation must be designed with versatility at the forefront to deliver sustainability. Schemes that maximize storage space and efficiency can be utilized to create comfortable and convenient living spaces on the tightest of plots, and architects and product designers are developing ever-more solutions. The integration of robotic and smart technology presents exciting new opportunities for innovation and provides a glimpse of the possible future of residential architecture. ●

[1] The bright and incredibly orderly apartment 5S, designed by Nicholas Gurney.

[2] Elie Metni's easy-to-clean Shoebox micro-unit in Beirut.

[3] HEIMA architects' micro-apartments in Vilnius, Lithuania.

[4] Yesul Jang's Tiny Home Bed, a compact storage solution.

[5] Nmstudio's versatile plywood pegboard walls offer clever storage and display solutions.

A tiny house atop a larger one

- CASA PARÁSITO
- EL SINDICATO ARQUITECTURA
- QUITO, ECUADOR

"Parasitic House," despite its title, is relatively self-contained—a budget-friendly, environmentally conscious living solution that means the young inhabitants do not have to relinquish independent living. Instead, their requirements are housed within a space of 129 square feet (12 square meters) on top of an existing building in the popular San Juan neighborhood of Quito.

Conceived as a "minimal design object," the A-frame structure is arranged around a central, rectangular core that is free of in-built structures, allowing the inhabitants to move around it freely. The functional modules—kitchen, shower, storage, sleeping area—are then tucked into the eaves and, in the case of the sleeping area, raised above head-height. This has the added advantage of stabilizing and strengthening the structure. Despite its minimal use of resources, there are, nevertheless, luxurious aspects to the house, with the northern facade, made up entirely of glass panels, offering a view of the city that would satisfy even the most demanding client.

Previous pages
The design is practical in its use of materials: a glass facade to the north offers wide-open views, while the frosted south facade brings privacy; the east and west facades are clad in steel to lessen the impact of direct sunlight.

Current pages
Interior walls, ceilings, and flooring are all lined with OSB panels—characteristic for their random wood-strip patterning. The panels are valued for their load-bearing qualities and work with the geometry of the structure to offer greater stability.

A city-center escape, designed for a modern couple

- RESORT IN HOUSE
- ALPES GREEN DESIGN & BUILD
- DA NANG, VIETNAM

In almost every space in this home one can see or feel the outdoors. Even the entry-level pool—a striking feature in its own right—is illuminated by light that drops down the central well from a louvered skylight three levels above. A central light well is common to many urban plots in East Asian cities, but here the effects are augmented by a system of perforated walls, indoor and outdoor planting, and a hanging garden-style, street-facing facade.

One floor contains only a bedroom, bathroom, and laundry room by way of functional spaces—yet each space is integral to the program of airflow and light movement operating through the house, making the intense Vietnamese climate feel comfortable. Even the rooftop garden has a part to play in absorbing intense, direct sunlight. The varied material palette deployed here—cast and polished concrete, timber, natural rock and stone, and, of course, brick—foregrounds natural materials with cooling properties, and also creates a soothing feel, akin to that of a spa or resort.

Previous pages
The west-facing brick facade has panels with perforations to allow ventilation, while reducing the penetration of direct sunlight.

Current pages
Natural light enters the house via skylights, open spaces, and vents in walls. The effect is to create an ever-changing mood in the rooms as the day passes from morning to night.

The rooms are linked via split-level transitions. This reduces the number of internal walls, allowing for beautiful vistas within the home.

At the east-facing end of the house runs a two-story concrete structure that supports a series of brick planters. The structure also protects the rear of the house from direct sunlight and provides a green patio space.

A weekend retreat with panoramic views

- NERIMA HOUSE
- ELDING OSCARSON
- TOKYO, JAPAN

This home occupies less than half of the plot on which it sits, because the preservation of the existing garden was a priority for owners and architects alike. On the ground floor a band of wraparound windows was placed close to the floor, providing views of the greenery and offering a grounding perspective that immerses the viewer in the natural surroundings.

The outward-looking emphasis of this weekend home has implications for privacy, especially as the bedroom and bathroom sit on the lowest level, with living space on the floor above. This "ground" floor is slightly sunken, however, creating a sense of seclusion. While there is generally an openness and fluidity to the plan—especially on the upper level—storage and private functions are also somewhat hidden away at the rear of the site. Counterintuitively, the most secluded part of the building is the roof terrace. For a visiting couple with grown children, however, the relaxed approach to space and the apartment's surroundings is just right.

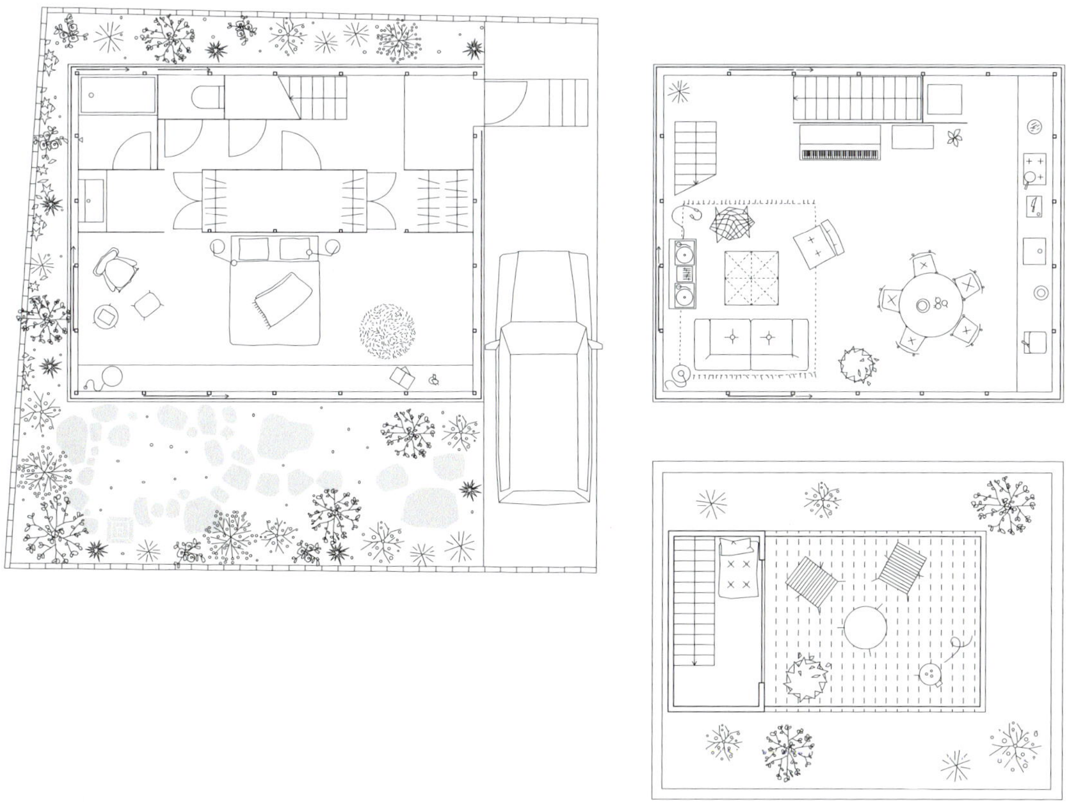

Previous pages
The spaciousness of the open-plan rooms is only emphasized by the band of wrap-around windows that winds along the entire house.

Current pages
With beautifully planted gardens on three sides and a terrace on the roof, the inhabitants are constantly surrounded by greenery.

A green sanctuary

- HOUSE 304
- KIENTRUC O
- HO CHI MINH CITY, VIETNAM

Situated in the busy Bình Thạnh District in central Ho Chi Minh City (HCMC), House 304, completed in 2015 by Kientruc O architects, is a light-filled home that fits a lot into a small footprint. The distinct recessed plan raises the building in three staggered levels, from a footprint of just 452 square feet (42 square meters), to a total of 1,851 square feet (172 square meters). The house includes living, dining, and kitchen areas on the ground floor; two bedrooms with outdoor access; three bathrooms; and a working area on the top floor. Its long and narrow form echoes the traditional Vietnamese town house, providing a haven of light and vegetation within a fast-paced urban setting.

The house "is an in-between buffer zone for nature and residents to live in harmony," the architects state. Lead architects Dam Vu and Anni Le wish to connect humans and nature in a reciprocal manner while also incorporating elements of Vietnam's local architecture.

The integrating element is the central light well, which brightens every level of the house. "As the opening gradually expands toward the sky in an oval-like well," the architects describe, "it allows light and air to fill the space, while breathing in a peaceful atmosphere across the house."

With "no rigid boundaries," the architects say, the space allows nature in "while maintaining the ability to create privacy and safety when necessary." Railings of slim vertical metal strips are lined along the edge of the well creating fluctuating shadows. On street level, an enclosed patio guards a lofty tree. And once inside, this is repeated with a second tree in the living room reaching up through the light well, blurring the distinction between outside and inside.

Although the house is situated in a residential area, the city is noisy, dense, and lacking green space. Therefore, the inclusion of greenery in the house is just as important as daylight. In contrast to the bright white walls and glossy ceramic floors, foliage is present and visible on every floor. And all materials, from the plants to the furniture, are locally sourced. The dark tropical wood furniture, custom-made by local carpenters, is built into the walls, maximizing space and circulation.

The facade, lined with perforated metal mesh, lets light into the house while shielding the main entrance from the street. The mesh further "protects the living space from direct sunlight from the west and softens the cubical rigidity of the typical town house."

While the house feels completely open, the floor plan doesn't sacrifice a sense of intimacy. Curtains may be closed at night, and sliding glass doors keep the cool temperature inside without compromising on the view. "The design context poses challenges to create a casual, well-ventilated, and well-lit space within a constrained building footage," the architects explain. "Vertical expansion of the light well helps to maximize the desired spatial quality." By creating a continuous relationship with the environment, the house provides a natural sanctuary within an urban core.

Previous pages A semitranslucent mesh wraps around the house at ground level, echoed in the railings on the balconies of the floor above. Each floor has its own garden.

Current pages At ground level the house is almost five times as long as it is wide; to the rear it opens up to reveal a light and airy double-height living room.

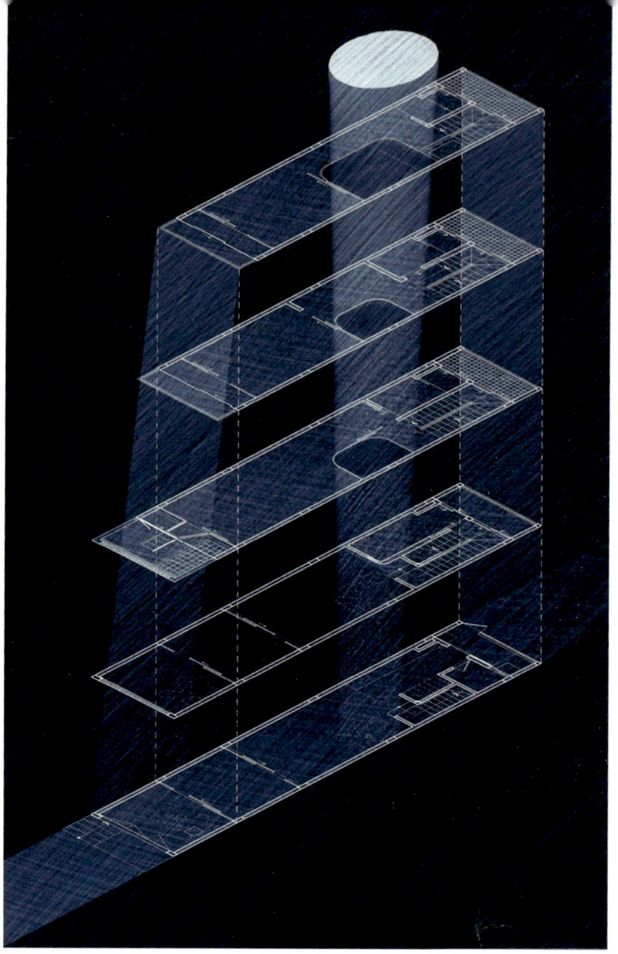

Throughout the rooms of the house, balconies, walls, and doorways feature rounded corners to match the oval lightwell.

48
46

Where the light shines down from above

- V19 RESIDENCE
- VIRAJE ARQUITECTURA
- CASTELLÓN DE LA PLANA, SPAIN

V19 Residence occupies a long, narrow site in the old town of Castellón de la Plana, Spain. While it is not uncommon for houses to be built on such sites, it is less usual for them to measure more than two stories high. In building taller, and with the longest walls being party walls—and so, windowless—the architects decided to bring light in from the top of the house and from the facade at the front. The design centers on the house having two internal courtyards and a skylight above the staircase, which cuts through the three floors of the house. The effect is to bathe all corners of the house in natural daylight. The main courtyard is covered with a glass ceiling and, although inside, it has been given an exterior treatment to give it the ambience of an outside space. Winding up through the center of the house, the staircase is a major feature of the design. Positioning it in the middle of the floor plan allowed the architects to make the most of the surrounding spaces as areas of use and circulation. Furthermore, it is paneled on both sides with micro-perforated steel, making it semi-transparent so that views across the whole width of the house can be taken in.

Previous pages
In a nod to the ceramic tradition of the province of Castellón, a skin-like latticework covers covers the facade. It filters light into the rooms, contributing to the play of light in the house.

Current pages
The first floor is used for day areas, where the living and dining room and the kitchen are connected by a covered patio with a glass floor.

The beauty of old things

- SAIGON HOUSE
- A21STUDIO
- HO CHI MINH CITY, VIETNAM

There's a real sense of fun and adventure in this house, which is created through the placement of a series of "floating" volumes between the bounding walls. They are connected by staircases, ladders, and even a large net floor, while color, texture, and the dappled light created by a patterned steel facade add to the overall feeling of lightness. It's no surprise that extended family life and children, in particular, were at the heart of the design concept.

Tiles, doors, and other elements of finishing were salvaged from old Saigonese houses that had been demolished, and the owners—turning away from the Western-style architecture that is increasingly common in the city—embraced traditional Vietnamese architectural forms like courtyards, alleyways, and balconies. The result is a balance of private rooms and open communal spaces with the intention for the house to be a place where the family can gather, socialize, and share memories.

Previous pages
Located in a narrow street in central Ho Chi Minh City, where it jostles with shopfronts and ramshackle buildings, the house looks as if it has been here for generations.

Current pages
Each of the floating volumes is a miniature house in its own right—some even have tiled pitch roofs—and strategic planting helps to blur the lines between inside and outside space.

An image of wandering

- HOUSE IN MINAMI-TANABE
- FUJIWARAMURO ARCHITECTS
- OSAKA, JAPAN

This project feels more like a concert hall or cultural center than a conventional home, and it underlines the primacy of light, movement, and space, even in a confined footprint. The architects conceived of the interior as a "landscape," with dramatic vistas and long sightlines, all tucked away behind the stainless-steel chain curtain that veils the facade, providing privacy while drawing the gaze away from the house's dense, industrial surroundings.

The building, on a plot measuring 12 by 56 feet (3.8 by 17 meters), has three main levels and a basement, but it gives the impression of even greater height as a result of split, staggered floors and huge light wells, which cut down through to the ground floor. The minimalism of the interior—timber flooring, white walls, and minimal fittings—is balanced by the drama of the huge, open staircases that connect the levels by a variety of routes, resisting the idea of monotonous movement. Only a basement bedroom, accessed via a hidden spiral staircase, contravenes the guiding principles of openness and visibility.

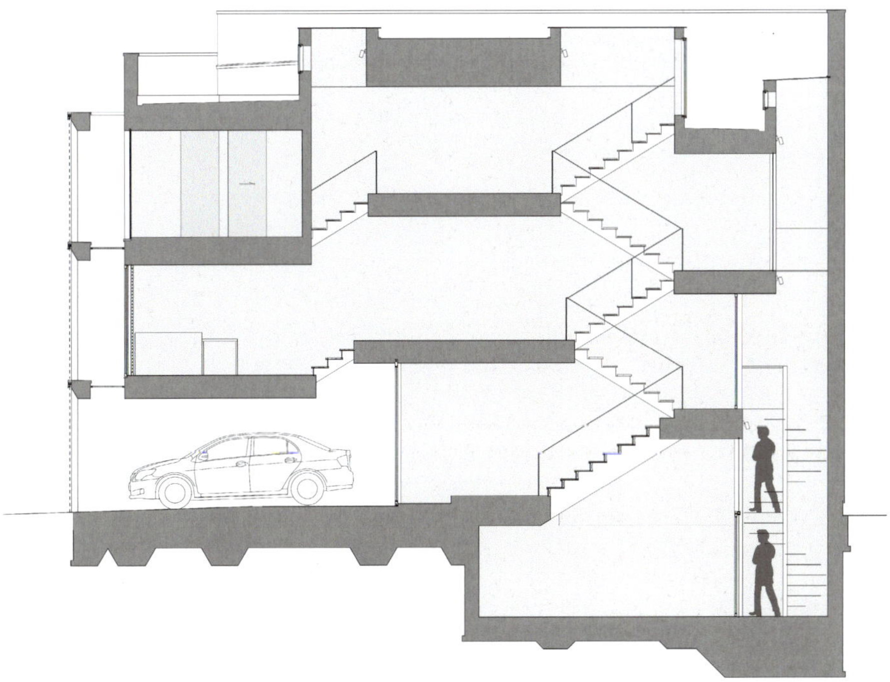

Previous pages
The architect describes the staircases as "scattered" in order to create multiple up-down circulation routes through the house, offering dynamic views of the interior.

Current pages
The architect's section drawing shows how staircases connect multiple levels.

A home that balances comfort and cool

- 3,500 MM HOUSE
- AGO ARCHITECTS
- SOUTH JAKARTA, INDONESIA

As its name suggests, this home is constrained in dimension, but it is finished in expressive style. Expanses of warm, polished wood—for facades, window frames, and fittings—along with carefully placed decorative touches belie the cost-efficient approach taken to design and construction. The inviting feel is achieved through careful management of light, which enters through skylights and is controlled by a perforated-steel screen that shields the street-facing facade.

A seating area in the first-floor living and dining room exemplifies the way comfort is expressed in this home without reducing function. Here, as elsewhere in the house, an extraordinary amount of storage is compressed into a tiny space, but the surfaces are plain and clean. The use of bespoke, “plug-in” furniture modules such as the seat and a children’s sleeping and study space on the third floor, recall the treatment of 13 m² House (see page 86); the result is practical yet clutter-free, and highly space-efficient.

Previous pages
Most of the natural light flooding into the rooms comes from the glass roof. A more diffuse light filters in through the perforated steel and polycarbonate facade.

Current pages
The rooms are full of plug-in storage solutions. In the living room, a coffee table doubles as bench seating and conceals a host of cupboards and drawers. There are even drawers between the stair treads.

A relaxed solution to limited living space

- 3 × 9 HOUSE
- A21STUDIO
- HO CHI MINH CITY, VIETNAM

In a home of this size—as the name suggests, it's on an unusually small plot, even for this notoriously dense city—the arrangement of individual elements takes on particular significance. Non-functional components of the plan, such as the slatted-wood terrace-style space on the first floor, must be weighed carefully for their advantages; in this case, the admittance of light to an almost windowless ground floor, and the creation of an outdoor-like space for clients who love nature are evidently worthwhile.

However, the efficiency required for such limited space has not translated into severity in this instance, where raw brickwork, a varied material palette, and indoor planting, which is common to many inner-city Vietnamese dwellings, create warmth and movement. Without room partitions, the architects have turned to solutions such as changes in floor level and bespoke fixtures and fittings to demarcate the various living spaces.

Previous pages
The facade, with its horizontal louvers and flourishes of vegetation, is distinctly contemporary. And yet, it perfectly mirrors the scale, colors, and textures of neighboring buildings.

Current pages
The ground floor combines three living areas in one long space: living room, dining room, and kitchen. The lack of partitions makes each one feel more roomy.

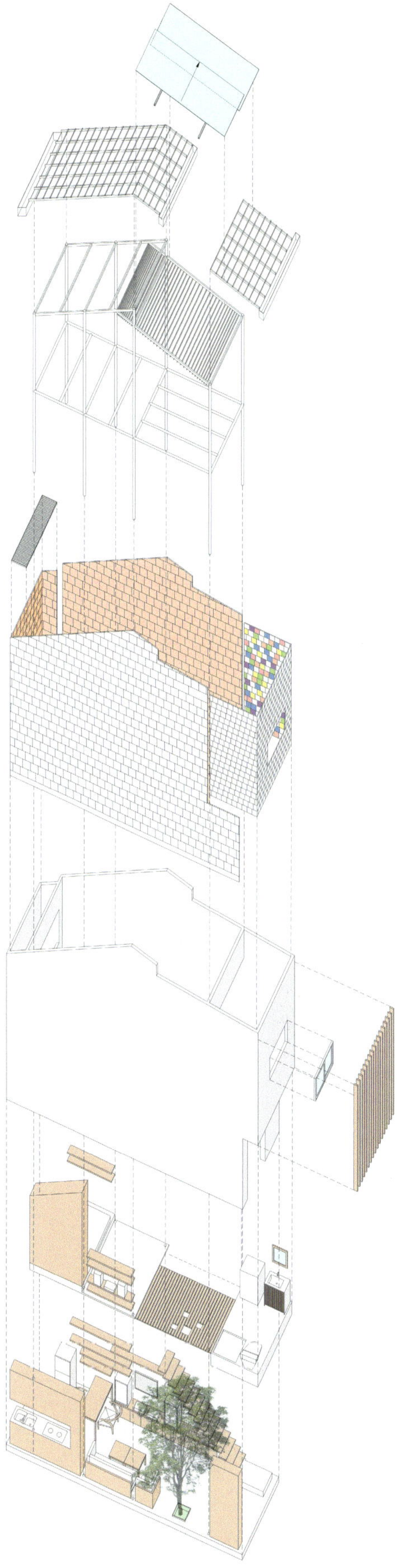

Two elements rise up from the ground floor to give this house an earthy, organic vibe: the rough-textured brickwork walls and the tree whose branches reach up to the skylight at the top of the house.

Architects choose the plot then shape the story

- HOUSE IN TEZUKAYAMA
- FUJIWARAMURO ARCHITECTS
- OSAKA, JAPAN

Squarely facing the street, but with asymmetric shapes and structures inside, this home in the dense neighborhood of Tezukayama is typical of the off-kilter buildings the architects are known for. They placed light and storage solutions literally at the center of this family home by integrating shelving and display spaces into the open structure of the pinewood staircase that twists up through the building. Beside the staircase is a series of glass-covered slits in the floor that allow light to filter down from apertures in the roof.

By incorporating storage space into this essential function (as well as in the "raised" ground floor, which conceals underfoot storage), the designers have freed up space in the four main living areas, which are arranged around the staircase, ascending from bedrooms and bathrooms to the living-dining-kitchen space and balcony on the top floor. The structurally independent stair column also provides seating and even two desk spaces, one of which is sized for the clients' young child. It is a creative and entirely bespoke feature that defines the house.

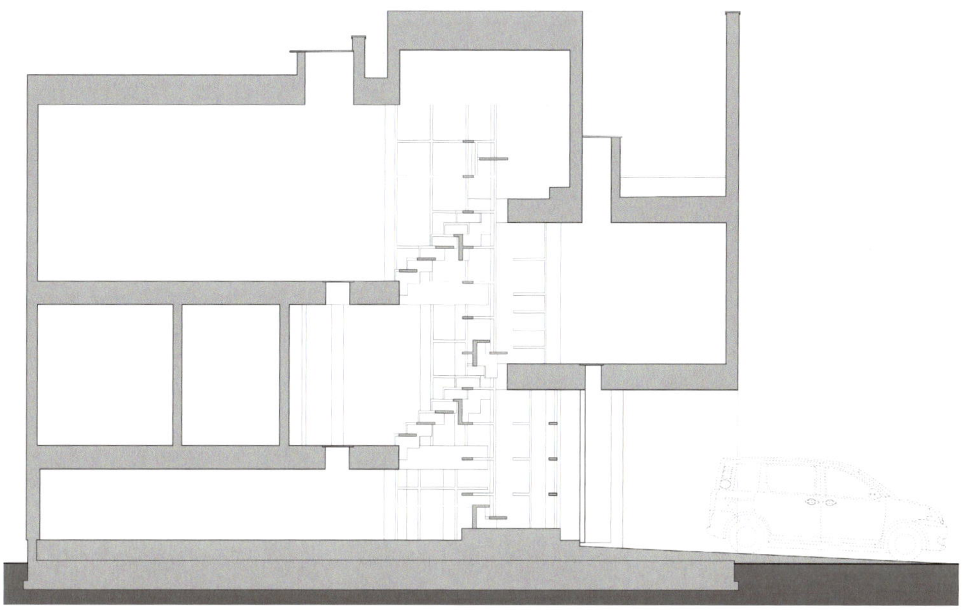

Previous pages
The raked angle of the entrance to the house and the slim apertures above seem to emphasize the narrowness of the facade.

Current pages
The openness of the pine structure allows light to filter in, creating what the architects describe as a "linked tube of light."

A labyrinth of light

- T NOIE
- KATSUTOSHI SASAKI + ASSOCIATES
- TOYOTA, JAPAN

The clerestory windows lining the top of this black box are, from the outside, almost the only chink in the "armor" of the dark painted-timber facades. The effect inside is a complete contrast—light streams down through the spiraling levels of the maze-like interior creating a "lightscape," to use the architect's description.

There are no stories in the traditional sense, but rooms are arranged over three levels, or zones. On the lower level are ground-floor living spaces and an interior garden. Above that, nestled into the middle level, are bedrooms and bathrooms. Next is the loft level, which features two more bedrooms and a study. Some areas of the plan are, however, full- or partial-height voids. The more meaningful division of the space is along the longitudinal axis: a central, semiporous core divides the numerous private spaces from the more open, airy segment of the house. It is the "T" created by this structure, in cross-section, that gives the home its name. The very narrow width of all the rooms means that supporting beams were not required, only the ubiquitous 2-inch (50-millimeter) plywood boards.

Previous pages
The house's rigidly geometric, 26-foot-tall (8-meter-tall) form is clad in dark-painted timber and topped with wraparound clerestory windows.

Current pages
A surprising amount of light floods in from the narrow band of windows at the top of the house, casting bright shafts deep into the rooms below.

The rooms are arranged on platforms set at varying heights around a spiral staircase, and the largely open-plan layout provides dynamic sight lines from the top of the building to the bottom.

A redefinition of the traditional Vietnamese lifestyle

- ANH HOUSE
- S+NA.
- HO CHI MINH CITY, VIETNAM

As with House 304 (see page 116), greenery is essential to this project, with 13 huge sunken planters dotted around the plan. However, in other respects, Anh House takes a completely contrasting approach to the "tube house" typology common in urban Vietnam. The focus here is on maximizing the movement of light and air through the four levels of the deep, narrow plot. The result is a home that appears to be almost see-through: light, woven-bamboo screens take the place of partition walls and can be pulled back to create open-plan living. Even the ground-level garage, sealed off in most homes, is divided from the living area by just a glass wall.

Huge voids and light wells open up the house vertically as well as horizontally. The top-level, in particular, is flooded with light. Inhabitants of the upstairs bedroom have the experience of waking up almost in the outdoors, with a view of the skyline. Further down the house, the dark, molded-concrete ceilings—echoing those traditional bamboo screens—provide the only grounding element.

Previous pages
On each level, the rooms are recessed to allow for an outdoor space overlooking the street. At night, architectural features such as the spiral staircase stand out against the dark ceilings.

Current pages
The open staircase works in tandem with holes punched in walls, floors, and ceilings to flood the house with natural light.

Pools of clear water and tropical plantings here and there combine to endow the house with a natural freshness and an ambience that is permanently cool and calm.

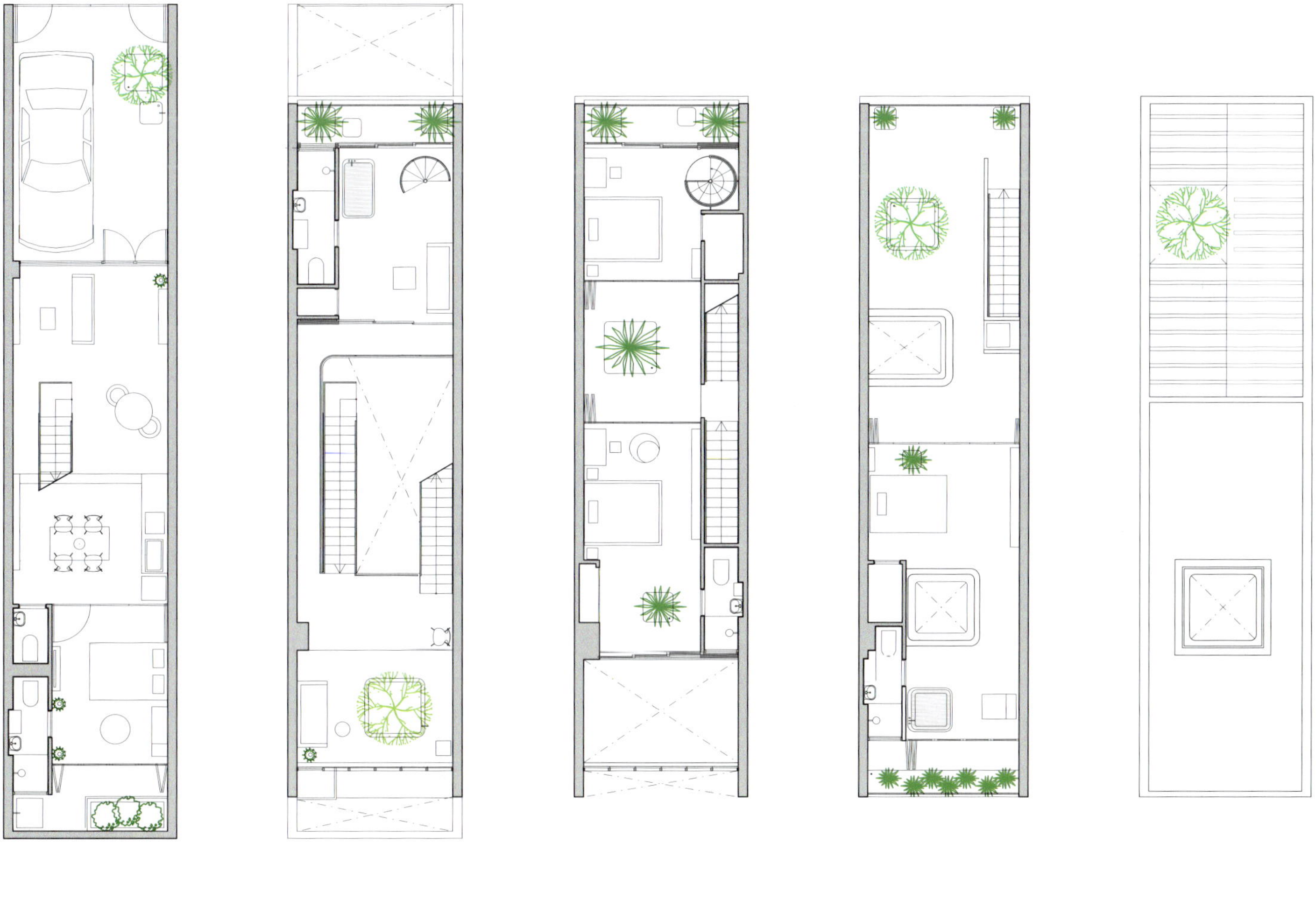

LIVING SMALL

As urban plots shrink in size, a look at traditional narrow homes around the world provides contemporary architects with inspiration and creative solutions for building with restricted space.

With a growing urban population and increasing real estate pressure, architects are developing inventive ways to squeeze homes into ever-smaller spaces. The compact housing trend is often presented as aspirational, seems compatible with the way young people tend to live now, and it delivers on expediency, and affordability. However, for many people around the world, cramped living conditions are an unavoidable necessity, in many cases incorporating both family and work.

> "For many, cramped living conditions are an unavoidable necessity, in many cases incorporating both family and work."

Ultranarrow homes often characterize the urban fabric of historic cities where the demand for housing has outstripped the supply of land, pushing developers and individuals to build on previously restricted, rejected, abandoned, or forgotten plots. This slender typology is particularly associated with densely populated cities in Japan, Vietnam, and the Netherlands, where small plots are particularly common, but the architectural solutions vary widely across different locations.

[1]

[2]

THE VIETNAMESE *HẺM*

The urban grid in the center of Ho Chi Minh City (HCMC) was largely shaped by French colonization in the 19th century. While French colonial architecture was employed for government and official buildings, the integration of boulevards and roundabouts that emulated French cities gave way to extensive city blocks, leaving many empty unclaimed lots in between.

Narrow passageways took shape to provide access to these lots, and, over time, communities built their homes along either side of them, blending private spaces with life on the streets. These alleyways are known as *hẻm,* and they are ubiquitous in HCMC, Da Nang, and Hanoi. Ranging from a mere 3.5 to 13 feet (1 to 4 meters) wide, a culture of intimacy envelops them, with inhabitants eating, sleeping, working, and playing in extreme proximity.

Most families living in a *hẻm* have lived in their homes for several generations, gradually adapting them according to their changing needs. Some noticeably mid-century modern details have been incorporated, such as perforated cement tiles or brick screens with openings that provide privacy and ventilation. Permeable facades and interspersed terraced volumes allow for much-needed ventilation in the tropical climate.

Recently, architects have been reconfiguring some of these properties to create lighter, more →

private dwellings without compromising on tradition. Sanuki Daisuke Architects' design for the single-family Hem House in the center of HCMC exemplifies this approach. In this instance, the corner plot allowed them to add generous openings along the perimeter wall, but others, like some of the projects by HCMC-based architects MM++ have introduced light wells that cut vertically through the center of the slim volumes allowing daylight to flood in from above.

MACHIYA SHOPHOUSES OF JAPAN

A similar narrow, multifunctional typology emerged in Kyoto during the 11th and 12th centuries when merchants and artisans conducted their business from properties with living quarters at the back. Commonly no more than two-stories high, *machiya,* as these wooden shophouses are known, often feature enclosed courtyards and gardens that divide the domestic spaces from the business premises. The outer walls usually consist of removable *kōshi* screens that easily transform the storefront.

> "*Mujō,* or impermanence, implies that homes are always subject to change and adaptability."

The Japanese concept of *mujō,* or impermanence, implies that homes are always subject to change and adaptability. While the Japanese culture tends to renew rather than restore, some initiatives, led primarily by architects, have involved refurbishing *machiya* and adapting them for modern-day life. One such example is a project by td-Atelier, together with Endo Shojiro, who remodeled and adapted a series of 120-year-old *machiya* in Kyoto to form guesthouses. The interior spaces employ traditional shoji screens and sliding doors that can be opened or closed as needed, making them versatile spaces that can be adapted for different activities.

The sophisticated principles of building on incredibly narrow plots can be traced back to the *sukiya-zukuri* style, which originated in the Edo period (1603–1868), and is associated with small, modest spaces constructed from natural materials. This style of building is just as relevant in the country today. Tadao Ando's Row House, or Azuma, in Osaka (1976) presents an austere concrete facade that conceals an open courtyard behind it. This type of architecture tends to have an unassuming appearance that slots in between existing buildings without being invasive or pretentious.

[3]

More recent examples of Japanese row houses include the 237-square-foot (22-square-meter) Love2 House by Takeshi Hosaka Architects, and a house just 6 feet (1.8 meters) wide by YUUA Architects & Associates, which features interspersed platform levels that create a surprising openness. Metal mesh connects one slab to the next, facilitating circulation while letting light and air flow through.

GRACHTENPANDEN IN THE NETHERLANDS

In the 17th century, a strong economy allowed the Netherlands to begin structuring a network of canals, or *grachten,* to facilitate commerce and transportation, and the densification of city centers began. In Amsterdam, narrow canal houses, known as *grachtenpanden,* were built along the edges of the main canals and came to define the local vernacular. Narrow plots of land were divided, and property owners had to adapt to strict zoning and taxation regulations imposed in response to overcrowding. Some of the houses doubled as places of business or warehouses, and others had workshops on the first floor and homes above. The tall, thin buildings have a variety of gable roofs in ornate neo-Renaissance or neo-Baroque styles, and like the *machiya* in Japan, often feature secret gardens or enclosed courtyards behind their facades.

While most of the original canal houses still stand, albeit some repurposed, developments like the Borneo-Sporenburg district in the Eastern Docklands of Amsterdam have taken inspiration from this housing typology. The forward-thinking Rotterdam-based architecture firm MVRDV, led by Winy Maas, was among the architects commissioned to design 60 low-rise dwellings among the 2,500 housing units. They built two private houses in 1999, Borneo 12 and 18. The former measures a mere 8.2 feet (2.5 meters) wide and the latter is 13.7 feet (4.2 meters) wide. Both dwellings have four levels and achieve a feeling of openness through alternating ceiling heights and outdoor views through verandas, balconies, and bay windows echoing the layout of the original *grachtenpanden.*

The Borneo-Sporenburg urban plan, developed by West 8, maximized private outdoor space through roof gardens and courtyards, and pedestrian access was prioritized to reduce the impact of car use. The familiarity of the low-rise buildings, with their contemporary design and proximity to water, delivered high-density homes in a way that pays homage to the historic row houses and demonstrates their influence in the present.

In Almere Poort, west of Amsterdam, Ana Rocha Architecture built a modern row house prototype in 2018. Rather than working within a particular infill site, Slim Fit is designed to be adapted to any city and any narrow lot, even suggesting the use of party walls as insulation. While the design is still in the prototype phase, it is intended to be a sustainable solution that could be replicated for urban infill spaces of any size or shape, providing comfortable living spaces with clever storage and sliding screens.

[4]

[5]

> "Narrow plots of land were divided, with regulations imposed in response to overcrowding."

The question of whether vernacular architecture from one region can successfully inform another style of architecture in a location across the globe remains open-ended, but it is clear that historical examples of infill and ultranarrow architecture can inform architects on the challenges of building small spaces and inspire cost-effective, low-impact solutions, which will become increasingly critical as urban environments strain to accommodate ever-increasing populations. ●

[1] Anh House, Ho Chi Minh City, Vietnam (see also, page 154).

[2] MM++ Architects' Vietnamese town house (see also, page 164).

[3] Atelier Luke's beautifully restored *machiya* house in Kyoto.

[4] The canal-front facade of MVRDV's Borneo 12 development in Amsterdam.

[5] Ana Rocha's Slim Fit house in Almere Poort, Netherlands.

A contemporary approach to a traditional typology

- TOWN HOUSE WITH A FOLDING-UP SHUTTER
- MM++ ARCHITECTS
- HO CHI MINH CITY, VIETNAM

The brief was simple—a "shophouse," with an open commercial space at ground level—but the site restrictions were the same as for many urban Vietnamese buildings on narrow, deep plots. MM++ responded with one especially eye-catching intervention: the single-timber shutter—an adaptation of traditional colonial designs—transforms the street-facing elevation and frames the shop entrance, which otherwise seems to flow into the rest of the house via an open staircase leading upwards.

In practice, there was an effort to differentiate the public and the personal, with bedrooms and bathrooms over the upper three levels oriented around a building-height void toward the back of the site. The kitchen-dining space on the ground floor opens out onto a small garden. The treatment of the family rooms also differs from the raw industrial materials utilized in the commercial section of the house, with warm wood and white polished surfaces favored over concrete and steel.

Previous pages
Seen from the street, the house feels comfortable in its surroundings; the linear textures of the timber shutter and rooftop pergola find echoes in the tiling and railings of neighboring houses.

Current pages
The open floor plan sees light flooding into all of the rooms from a large skylight toward the back of the house.

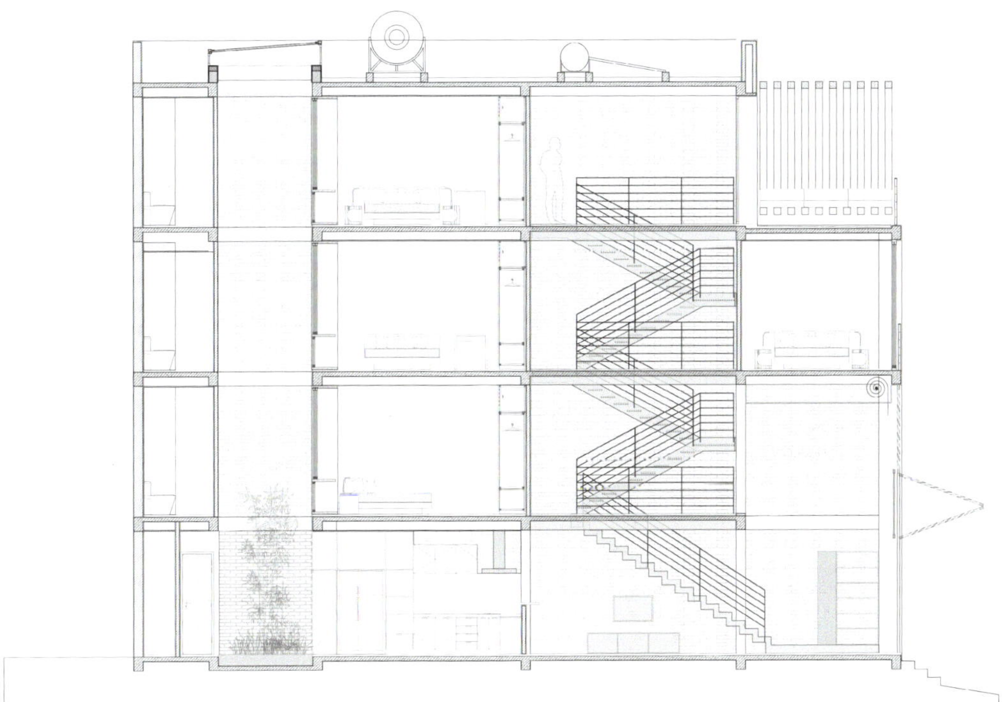

Lining the wall that flanks the staircase, glazed brick tiles rise up from the commercial space through all floors of the house and even the rooftop terrace.

Bringing the outdoors in

- PIRAJÁ HOUSE
- ESTÚDIO BRA ARQUITETURA
- SÃO PAULO, BRAZIL

The owners—third-generation members of a São Paulo family—have replaced the somewhat dilapidated row house that once stood on this street with a tiny but warm and welcoming home. The only physical element that has been retained in the new building are a number of structural brick walls. Visually in keeping with the surrounding architecture, the low ceilings and limited natural light in the original property have been replaced with a smaller but brighter and more open living space.

In contrast to projects such as the House in Minami-Tanabe (see page 130), here the architects have embraced private spaces, conventional room arrangements, and even "clutter" in the form of fittings, furniture, and visible structural features. Careful attention to the flow of movement around the home has imbued the new layout with a dynamic feel. The garden entrance, internal courtyard, outdoor kitchen, and roof terrace—incorporating a vegetable garden and relaxing outdoor space—bring the outdoors inside. Full-height windows in each of the main rooms enhance the airy, outward-looking atmosphere.

Previous pages
Despite its very contemporary elevation and increased height, the new house remains unobtrusive when viewed from across the street.

Current pages
On the ground floor, the front and end walls are almost entirely glass. Opened up, they extend the living space considerably—out toward the street and into the courtyard garden at the rear.

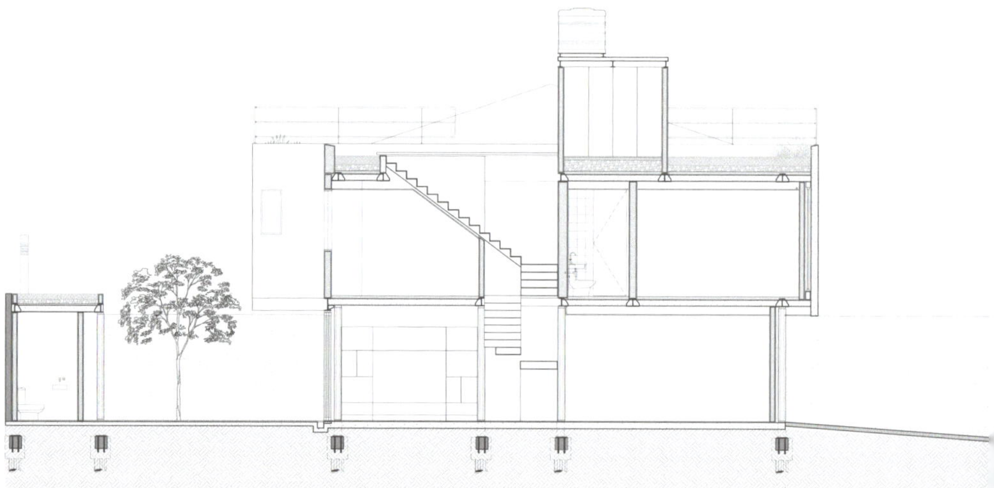

By converting the roof into a slab garden and planting a mature tree in the central garden below, the architects have introduced welcome green spaces to the development.

A former parking spot becomes a thriving London home

- POCKET HOUSE
- TIKARI WORKS
- LONDON, U.K.

Once the site of an old car garage in East Dulwich, London, Pocket House is a quintessential example of adaptability in the limited footprint of an urban infill. The single-family dwelling was designed by husband-and-wife duo Nicola and Ty Tikari, of London-based architecture firm Tikari Works. They worked within the bounds of just 883 square feet (82 square meters), rethinking the traditional layout of Western homes by turning it "upside-down"—living and kitchen areas are situated above ground, while the bedrooms are sunken underground.

Completed in 2018, the timber screen-lined home is set back from the street to align with neighboring residences, which typically feature front yards. "The screen borrows its language from wooden garages and garden sheds, helping to contextualize the building and harmonize the facade as a sculptural 'whole,'" the Tikaris say. While providing space for a front courtyard and privacy from the street, the recess of the house further allowed space for a sunken patio, which also serves as a light well for the two bedrooms on that level. Throughout the house, the architects opted for floor-to-ceiling windows and full-height sliding glass doors, "creating an arrangement of solid and void, which helps to create unity between the limited outdoor space and internal spaces."

Skylights also play a significant role. An opening above the kitchen area floods the neutral brick wall (painted in a tone that mimics the wood throughout) with natural light and provides a feeling of spaciousness above. Likewise, the sculptural staircase allows light to filter through the gaps between each timber step while sunlight pours through the seamless glass ceiling.

Visual accents provide intriguing perspectives inside the house. "Oversized doors and folding walls," the architects explain, are part of their way to "further play with expectations and sense of space, offering a more generous experience." As part of the plan, two independent volumes were devised as individual "pods," creating a trompe l'oeil effect of thick *poché* walls that conceal built-in furniture elements like desks and storage space, as well as the two bathrooms.

The floors are kept simple with polished concrete on the first two levels and wide wooden planks on the top floor where the living room's open plan makes for a welcoming ambiance. The ceilings in the bedrooms are shot-blasted concrete, while the ceilings in the top two levels are clad with timber beams for a warm, natural look. "This bold use of materials creates spaces that are visceral and legible," and as the architects note, "It was all achieved on a limited budget to create a family home that has a lasting quality over time."

The Tikaris see the whole process as "turning project constraints into design opportunities." This was the first project designed by Nicola and Ty Tikari as a team, and they also took on the roles of client and contractor. As they see it, "Pocket House demonstrates how good design can radically transform even the smallest of spaces."

61D

Previous pages
Above ground, the house steps back to align with neighboring building lines to the front and to limit impact to neighboring gardens to the rear.

Current pages
Inside and out, the materials employed borrow from the language of domestic garages and garden sheds: the wooden screen of the facade and the bare brickwork and mellow timber of the internal spaces.

Oversized doors, floor-to-ceiling windows, and frameless skylights conjure light, bright rooms, and a generosity of space.

COMPACT HOUSING EXPERIMENTS

Visionary architecture that takes advantage of under-utilized urban spaces may offer solutions to a global shortage of affordable housing.

Although the response to the global housing shortage remains critically underdeveloped, creative architectural proposals are revolutionizing the way we think about shelter. By the year 2050, it is projected that 70% of the world's population will live in cities, and three billion people will be living without adequate shelter. At the same time, real estate prices have skyrocketed due to the lack of subsidized housing, and "urban gigantism," which refers to the dominance of cities, has proliferated.

As homeownership in densely packed yet highly desirable cities becomes increasingly inaccessible, architects and designers have begun to reconsider prefab, mobile, and parasitic homes that cling onto existing structures. In combination with inventive designs for infill lots, these postwar concepts offer solutions to the lack of space in metropolitan environments and can be exploited to provide an antidote to poor-quality housing at a time defined by the climate emergency and refugee crises.

PREFAB ARCHITECTURE

From concrete pipeline tubes designed for stacked living to 3D printers that can print a home on-site within 24 hours, prefab architecture can offer an economical way of tackling homelessness.

In 1953 the influential French-Hungarian architect and urban planner Yona Friedman proposed an idea for cylindrical shelters made of pipeline material integrated with a natural cooling system for their use in hot climates. Fast-forward to 2017, when Hong Kong architect James Law of Cybertecture designed a social housing prototype called OPod Tube House. Law says these "starter homes" are meant for young residents. They can be stacked to form communities with shared co-living spaces, and they could also serve as transitional homes to alleviate the housing crisis, for example, on the public piers of Hong Kong's Central District or on top of cargo barge ships. Whether a two-person tube home is conducive to physical and mental health is yet to be tested, but Law hopes that by forming communities around these tubes with shared amenities and public space, residents will discover the benefits of communal living.

[1]

[2]

> "The social enterprise addresses youth homelessness by providing studio homes for families' backyards."

Another example of prefab architecture comes from Australian-based Grimshaw Architects. The Peak, completed in 2018, has a 350-square-foot (32.5-square-meter) footprint and was commissioned by Nestd for the not-for-profit organization Kids Under Cover. This social enterprise addresses youth homelessness by providing studio homes for families' backyards. (Nestd even offers to buy back the home when no longer needed.) The program has proven successful, and with Grimshaw's design, which includes a composting toilet, solar panels, high ceilings, and a contemporary design aesthetic, the program neatly combines affordability with sustainability.

Another project tackling homelessness is the Lighthouse 1.0 micro-dwelling created by all (zone), a design studio based in Bangkok. Intended to provide temporary shelters for homeless people →

in countries with tropical climates, the designers describe Lighthouse 1.0, as "an attempt to create a new type of domestic space in a tropical metropolis." The structure takes the form of a white wire mesh cube with fabric partitions "instead of the generic [rigid] housing type," a solution that they hope may be adapted and easily transported for nomadic or displaced users.

ICON, an advanced construction technologies company based in Austin, Texas, has teamed up with the homebuilding not-for-profit New Story to tackle the noxious conditions of informal housing with the first 3D-printed concrete housing community in Tabasco, Mexico (structurally engineered for the earthquake-prone state). Once completed, it will consist of 50 two-bedroom homes that offer residents a higher standard of living and the opportunity to develop a new community.

[4]

INFILL SITES

Intelligent designs for constricted alleyways and irregular plots that integrate outdoor space and natural light can maximize their potential to provide single- or multi-family homes that don't compromise on quality of life for residents.

Greenfill Housing as Garden, a finalist project in Big Ideas for Small Lots, a housing design competition organized by New York City in 2019, is one such proposal for a narrow site in Manhattan designed by the late architect Michael Sorkin. The volume is set back from the street to allow for staggered terraces on the facade with flow-planters on each of the seven units, providing outdoor spaces for the residents and increasing the level of daylight inside. There is a "hotel room" on the top-level that residents can use for hosting family or guests.

[3]

A similar project, located in Brooklyn, New York, by Only If Architecture, is a prototype for a narrow house on an overlooked plot, just 12.8 feet (3.9 meters) wide. Floor-to-ceiling windows, split levels, and metal mesh staircases ensure that daylight floods the property and makes it feel more spacious than it is. Backed by MINI Living, the architects hope it will serve as a prototype for other residual sites.

PARASITIC ARCHITECTURE

Most parasitic structures are either conceptual or have been built as short-term accommodation, and while some examples stem from a critique on homelessness and land speculation, it is clear that parasitic architecture could provide much-needed affordable inner-city housing.

One of the movements most influential on contemporary parasitic architecture is that of the Metabolists, a group of Japanese architects who addressed housing issues after the Second World War by thinking of buildings as living organisms and incorporating flexible modules. Among these architects was Kiyonori Kikutake, whose tree-like steel frame Landmark Tower designed for the Osaka Expo '70 used the principles of a living organism with parasitic geodesic capsules designed to be individual dwellings. Architect Kishō Kurokawa's Takara Beautilion, a jungle gym-like structure that could be infinitely expanded, was also exhibited at the same event.

> "Quadrangle Architects proposed attaching prefab homes to the CN Tower in Toronto, a project they deemed 'a sustainable and conscientious idea with minimal impact.'"

Following in the footsteps of the Metabolists, Toronto-based Quadrangle Architects proposed attaching modular prefab condo homes to the wings of the 1976 CN Tower in Toronto, a project they deemed "a sustainable and conscientious idea with minimal impact." The wooden pods could be designed with various layouts and would offer residents a highly desirable city-center location with unparalleled views. The scheme could be adapted for other freestanding structures in locations where space comes at a premium.

[5]

Casa Parásito, a 129-square-foot (12-square-meter) prototype designed for one or two people by El Sindicato Arquitectura, also provides a template for future developments. Placed on the roof of an existing building in central Quito, Ecuador, four structural timber A-frames maximize the interior space, which includes a bathroom, kitchen, bed, storage, and study areas. While the house could be placed in a rural or urban area, the architects propose that "its construction should occur on underused rooftops of urban structures."

In 2016, French architect Stéphane Malka designed and built a set of "democratic houses" called 3BOX, with a similar approach. The apartments are cantilevered between two existing buildings on a corner plot on the edge of the River Seine in Paris. "Building on rooftops is not only an ecological and economical solution," Malka says of his 40%-below-market-price housing, "It's working against the type of urban sprawl that kills the social link." Stacked one on top of the other, the modular steel, wood, and glass constructions each have private outdoor space and can be expanded depending on the residents' needs.

Some of these ideas may seem radical and, perhaps, to a certain extent, unrealistic, but without bold experimentation and unconventional ways of increasing the provision of cost-effective accommodation in highly populated cities, it will be impossible to tackle the severe housing shortage. Rather than expanding cities, prefab, infill, and parasitic architecture work with existing structures and available lots, minimizing the carbon footprint of developments while addressing the lack of adequate shelter, which makes them promising solutions for the future. ●

[1] ICON is exploring the concept of 3D-printed houses; this example is in Mexico.

[2] Only If Architecture's narrow prototype house in Brooklyn.

[3] Stéphane Malka's *Self Defense* installation at the Arche de la Défense Paris.

[4] Stéphane Malka's 3BOX democratic housing design in Paris.

[5] Quadrangle's Parasitic CN Tower in Toronto sees the tower covered in wooden residential pods.

A blended live-work space not to be missed

● SARUGAKU PLURAL DIRECTED TOWER
● MASATOSHI HIRAI ARCHITECTS ATELIER
● TOKYO, JAPAN

You would be forgiven for looking twice at this slim, angular building on its unusual, tapering plot. It appears so singular as to be almost unbelievable, with its see-through, glass-paneled lower levels, irregular facades above, and a floating staircase leading to the skinny entry facade. Other ingenious eccentricities are hidden from view and make a virtue of the sloped plot: sloping floor plates generate space for under-floor storage, staggered floor levels, and extensive sound insulation.

The mixed-use building comprises a multifamily house, shop, and small office, with workspaces found in the interstices between these functions, the intention being that work and home life will blend entirely. The "fragmentation" of living this represents is softened by the architect's extensive use of timber, sourced in Japan. Indeed, the interior feels warm and deceptively spacious, with simplicity being the watchword in the open, largely unfurnished spaces.

Previous pages
Impossibly thin at its entranceway, the building widens to mirror the footprint of its corner plot.

Current pages
From above, it is clear how the house becomes both taller and wider as it recedes from its narrowest point. Decked balconies and rooftop terraces (opposite) provide all-important outside space where otherwise there would be none.

Interiors are bright and spacious, rendered in natural materials, such as polished concrete floors and the warm timber elements used throughout.

APOLLO ARCHITECTS & ASSOCIATES

In densely populated Japan, Apollo Architects' houses poetically plug into their context—and aren't afraid to stand out in the crowd.

クロネコヤマトの
宅急便

Apollo Architects & Associates' slender homes slot into the world's most populous city like puzzle pieces. In Japanese cities like Tokyo, where Apollo's team lives among 37 million other inhabitants, land is limited and expensive. Building plots tend to be small, but lead architect Satoshi Kurosaki explains that small spaces are not necessarily considered unfavorable. "Japanese people tend to associate small spaces with spirituality and, therefore, often prefer modest homes," the architect says, adding that he believes modest spaces are conducive to "appreciating every element."

"They have developed several inventive strategies that shield residents from view without diminishing the natural light available inside."

Kurosaki grew up in Kanazawa, a city known for its beautifully preserved Edo period (1603–1868) temples and historic *bukeyashiki* samurai residences. Kurosaki studied architecture at Meiji University, and in 2000, established Apollo Architects & Associates in Tokyo, specializing in bespoke residential projects across Japan. His design approach can be traced back to traditional Japanese dwellings known as *machiya* and *nagaya* (town house and row house, respectively).

The humble facades of Apollo's discrete homes integrate perfectly with their surroundings and offer residents a peaceful respite from the bustling city streets. Privacy is of utmost importance in these densely packed neighborhoods, which is reflected throughout their portfolio of over 150 residences. They have developed several inventive strategies that shield residents from view without diminishing the natural light available inside. Screens, wooden louvers, enclosed courtyards, and elevated windows are common exterior features, while overhanging or cantilevered volumes increase the living space. Open-plan layouts, efficient use of space, and a restrained palette of materials characterize the interiors.

Structure and Beauty

Apollo has demonstrated an extraordinary ability to deliver homes with a spaciousness that belies the reality of their dimensions. Sept, one of their first private residences, was designed for a family of four in Tokyo. Completed in 2009, the asymmetric, cantilevered steel and timber structure raised on *pilotis* is typical of Apollo's work. Exposed rafters cast an ever-changing pattern of light and shadow across the walls, marking the passage of time. Double-height windows overlook an enclosed courtyard filling the interiors with natural light and creating a sense of connection to the outdoors without compromising the family's privacy. The elegant open-tread spiral staircase at the center of the property echoes the pattern of the rafters, and the restrained gray and white color scheme, applied throughout, makes for a peaceful atmosphere.

Another example, Swing, is a three-story dwelling on a 495-square-foot (46-square-meter) plot. To make the brief even more challenging, the client requested that the home incorporate space for a carport. The result is a cantilevered form, which allows the upper floors to benefit from more floor space. The trapezoid-shaped structure with irregularly placed openings conceals its airy interiors. On the ground level, a car easily slots in beneath the first floor. →

Arrow
A characteristic feature of this house is its lack of symmetry. The off-set pitch of the roof allows for a slim skylight on the peak, which casts dramatic shadows on the walls within.

Swing (this page)
Building constraints in Tokyo left Swing's street-facing facade shaped like a trapezoid and with randomly placed windows.

Lattice (opposite)
The building's glass facade is obscured by a wall of wooden louvers.

Similarly, the scheme for Lattice incorporates space for the owner's car, and the structure, built on a long, narrow site, is raised on load-bearing concrete *pilotis*, the iconic stilt-like columns popularized by Le Corbusier. The street-facing facade of Lattice is completely covered with a dark wooden screen formed by wooden louvers, which lets natural light in while preserving the residents' privacy in the densely populated residential area. The staircase at the center of the house is completely open, with a delicate handrail and hollow risers, maintaining a visual connection between the front and rear of the house and a sense of uninterrupted space. Split levels between the first and third floors add to the surprisingly voluminous feel. Natural light pours in from openings in the roof, penetrating all three levels of the building, and the interiors are finished with a minimal industrial palette of exposed concrete and dark wood evoking a contemplative ambiance.

Boundless Luminescence

Serpiente is a five-story building renovation project that Apollo completed in 2010. There is a maximum of just 300 square feet (28 square meters) per floor—the fifth floor is the smallest at 172 square feet (16 square meters), and it includes a terrace and a green roof. "The challenge was creating an expansive feeling in such a limited space," Kurosaki says. The bathroom and shower are enclosed with transparent floor-to-ceiling glass so that it doesn't feel confined, and built-in storage space and furniture makes the most of the space available. The impression of spaciousness is accentuated by mirrors and, in contrast to many of Apollo's other projects, large street-facing windows, but only on the uppermost levels to preserve privacy inside.

"The challenge was creating an expansive feeling in such a limited space."

The L-shaped plan of Jewel, which was designed for an architect, his partner, and their child in 2018, is only 4.6 feet (1.4 meters) wide on its smallest side and fits snugly beside a similarly narrow house. The black cladding contrasts with both the neighboring properties and the unexpectedly luminous interior. Private spaces, such as the bedrooms and bathrooms, are on the ground floor and the open-plan living and working space is on the top floor. A glazed courtyard is seamlessly cut into the upper level, and the same gray tiles are used inside and out to blur the boundary between them.

Arrow, completed in 2013, is tucked in behind the owner's parents' home on a tiny plot. A gently sloping steel staircase provides access to the second-floor entrance. Adjoining the staircase is a diagonal wall that adds a dramatic sculptural element to the angular facade. Inside, a long clerestory window meets the sharply pitched ceiling above the open-plan kitchen and living space, filling it with natural light. On the ground floor, there is a photography studio, accessed through full-height glass sliding doors. The white walls are complemented by pale wood and cream-colored ceramic tile floors throughout, while bold black accents provide a counterpoint and add definition to the minimalist space.

Sophisticated details are key to Apollo's impactful yet understated approach. "I try to restrict the number of materials to establish a minimal aesthetic," Kurosaki says. "Small architecture only works when the details are impeccable." ●

Sept
Austere, angular facades with cantilevered volumes and minimalist monochrome interiors are recurring characteristics in Apollo's work.

archium
2016

Minimum space, maximum impact

- MAXMINIMUM
- ARCHIUM ARCHITECTS
- SEOUL, SOUTH KOREA

An arrestingly simple presence on the streets of Seoul, this exposed concrete monolith is immediately notable because it is extremely narrow. The exterior features a covered entryway that forms an adjoining terrace, and the translucent polycarbonate curtain walls on the side facades add to the dramatic impression created by the street-facing elevation. Inside, the space is just as uncompromising, with surfaces limited almost entirely to concrete and plasterboard. The simple, linear layout proceeds from the ground floor, up past the minimal kitchen, and on to the bedroom and study on the top level.

On a site just 13 feet (4 meters) wide, with a section only 6.5 feet (2 meters) wide available for construction, the possibilities were undoubtedly constrained. In response, the architects focused on light and movement through the site. The incorporation of details like the cutout volumes in the exterior and balcony areas incorporated into the footprint show that human experience can be privileged even in a restricted space. The architects explain that the fixtures and fittings are muted to promote a "sense of space."

Previous pages
From the street, the polycarbonate skin almost takes on the appearance of polished marble, precision carved to accommodate the niches.

Current pages
Inside the house, the illusion of space is maintained to some extent by varying the ceiling heights across the floors.

Opposite
Vertical divisions, as well as horizontal ones, make for more dynamic views across the house.

This page
Materials have been chosen purposefully in order to limit any sense of clutter: frameless glass screens; texture-free work surfaces; and wooden doors that are free of paneling or molding.

A radically narrow home in central Tokyo

- 1.8-METER-WIDTH HOUSE
- YUUA ARCHITECTS & ASSOCIATES
- TOKYO, JAPAN

This steel-frame building was erected on a plot just 6.5 feet (2 meters) wide, the Japanese legal minimum—a person with their arms extended could touch both interior sidewalls. With no partition walls, a street-facing facade made almost entirely of glass, and gaps between the floating floor plates, the architects have created openness and fluidity in the constrained space. Clever hidden strategies such as the use of natural ventilation to avoid a bulky air-conditioning system free up even more living space for the single resident.

The interior is minimal yet rich and warm, with matte black walls and warm wooden floors and ceilings. This aesthetic is held in balance with surprising structural features such as changes in floor level and charming touches like the steel staircase with individually shaped steps and a hidden ladder between floors. There is a sense that the house is to be discovered, with, as the designers put it, "occasions forging individuality and personality."

川上工業所

Previous pages Squeezed into a gap in a busy central Tokyo street, this narrow house marks a distinct departure from the neighboring buildings.

Current pages Each story in the house is long and open-plan; split levels add a new dynamism and help to define areas for different uses.

This page
A spiral staircase winds up three floors at the rear of the house; some of the treads extend along the wall to create shelving.

Opposite
The split levels create exciting views through what would otherwise be fairly plain boxlike spaces. There is a tremendous sense of flow and movement.

Fluid spaces in a blank-canvas home

- IMAI
- KATSUTOSHI SASAKI + ASSOCIATES
- OKAZAKI, JAPAN

A liberated vision of flexible, hyper-modern living, or the endgame of relentlessly open-plan, minimal design? It all depends on your perspective in this uncompromising but thoughtful Japanese home. Safe to say, it's not for those who love clutter.

Despite the seeming purity of expression, the architects argue that there is no overarching concept, rather a set of principles governing the use of scale and light, for example. The layout prioritizes "lines of flow" rather than conventional room division and use, and barring the kitchen and bathroom, the rooms are multipurpose: a hallway becomes an office, the dining room becomes a bedroom, and freedom of movement is absolute. Light is concentrated in the gathering spaces, like the dramatic double-height living space on the first floor and the "indoor garden" on the ground level, while heat is funneled up through the building so it can escape through roof-level windows. An enclosed terrace on the second floor offers an unsullied glimpse of the sky.

駐車お断り

Previous pages
Raised on *pilotis* and with the first floor recessed, the house has no conventional features from the street view—no door, no windows—and resembles a storage container more than a family home.

Current pages
Long, clean lines, stark geometry, and minimalist, multiuse living spaces are the hallmark of the abode's interior.

INTERFACE STUDIO ARCHITECTS

Philadelphia studio ISA got their start slotting multi-unit homes into the awkward vacant lots that were dotted throughout the city center

CHOI
FUNERAL HOME
CHOI FUNERAL HOME, INC
215-629-1923
CHOI
FUNERAL HOME
NO STOPPING
ANY TIME
FOUNDER
JAYSON P. CHOI
THE ONLY
CHINESE-VIETNAMESE
LICENSED
FUNERAL DIRECTOR
FUNERAL HOME IN
PENNSYLVANIA

Brian Phillips and Deb Katz formed Interface Studio Architects (ISA) in 2005, just three years before the 2008 housing crash. At the time, American cities were attracting a new generation of city dwellers, so ISA responded with a series of projects that challenged existing urban living standards. The duo noticed that young people were moving to core urban neighborhoods fueling dynamic art, music, and food scenes, which in turn led to new development. Since then, ISA has been instrumental in revitalizing these districts, particularly in Philadelphia, where the studio is based.

> "Part of our design approach is to embrace radically pragmatic design solutions and then amplify their expression through formal, material, and pattern moves."

"When the city experienced disinvestment during the second half of the 20th century (mainly due to redlining and segregation), it lost a quarter of its population and tens of thousands of vacant lots appeared," Phillips explains. Later, when reinvestment began, most of the new residential developments were built in the "least challenging" lots, leaving behind an array of inconsistent land openings throughout the city that were frequently used as parking spaces. "Part of our design approach," Phillips adds, "is to embrace radically pragmatic design solutions and then amplify their expression through formal, material, and pattern moves." Three of their recent residential projects: Tiny Tower, El Chalet, and XS House exemplify this strategy. They were all built on constrained plots and provide proof that progressive architecture can be a force for positive change in marginalized urban locations.

Tiny Tower

Constructed in 2018, this five-story home, dubbed Tiny Tower, is less than 13 feet (4 meters) wide and stands on a narrow back street between two parking lots in Philadelphia's Brewerytown neighborhood. The metal-panel facade offers a striking contrast to the brick row houses surrounding it.

ISA optimized its vertical circulation to make the most of the plot's size limitations, which included zoning restrictions on height. Large staggered windows offer an intriguing glimpse into the stairwell, which is placed at the front of the building rather than down one side or spiraling up in a corner, the tradition for Philly houses.

Each level is designed for a specific function—there is one room on each floor (not counting bathrooms) and a roof terrace on the top. The windows provide abundant natural light, and simple light strips along the corners and ceilings offer ambient light that washes down the white walls. Clean lines and minimal furnishings make the narrow rooms feel spacious.

The tower's affordability—costs totaled $265,000 (€224,000)—was achieved, in part, because the plot faces a "secondary street," typically used for parking or backyards. Also, its size made it unsuitable for market-standard house plans. Tiny Tower was built between two parking lots, but ISA's design deliberately incorporated blind lateral walls, anticipating future development. Aside from spatial innovation, Phillips asserts that "the project is about affordability and modesty and thinking about how people should be living in the present and future." As such, it's a successful prototype for prospective development in Philadelphia and beyond. →

Tiny Tower
Offset or mis-matched windows are a common feature of ISA's designs. They offer intriguing views into the house from the outside, but also allow for the more creative use of the spaces within.

El Chalet

The zigzagging roof line picks up on the randomness of the surrounding architecture. Bright orange highlights in the facade repeat in the apartments within to tie the interior and exterior of the building together.

El Chalet

Like Tiny Tower, El Chalet, built in 2014, needed to comply with strict zoning laws, but the plot's proximity to an elevated train track added a further challenge. In response to these constraints, the architects turned the 6-unit apartment building sideways, meaning that the narrow front elevation is street-facing. Phillips explains that El Chalet, located in an undervalued and neglected neighborhood adjacent to a vacant lot, "exemplifies our interest in developing design ideas out of mundane parameters." The idiosyncratic four-story scheme borrows from the roofs of neighboring buildings to form an eye-catching asymmetric silhouette. The roofline incorporates several creative solutions, such as covered bicycle parking, staggered decks, and stormwater drainage. In each unit, ISA prioritized the human experience by providing private outdoor space for residents. Inside, natural sunlight pours in through large south-facing windows.

> "We're not afraid to use the vocabulary of developers, lawyers, and marketing consultants to help impact the broader development vision and attainability."

Projects like El Chalet help to realize the potential of "leftover" plots of land—a growing priority in cities where land is increasingly limited. "We're not afraid to use the vocabulary of developers, lawyers, and marketing consultants to help impact the broader development vision and attainability," asserts Phillips.

XS House

Another example of reviving a forgotten pocket of urban land is ISA's impossibly narrow seven-unit apartment building, XS House. In the 1950s, the gargantuan 10-lane Vine Street Expressway was built, splitting several Philadelphia neighborhoods in two. This includes Chinatown, which is still scattered with irregularly shaped blocks and empty lots.

Measuring 11 by 93 feet (3.4 by 28.3 meters), this six-story block, built in 2019, stands right on the edge of the highway. The intelligent design uses overhanging volumes to increase the living space available on the slender plot. Charcoal-colored fiber cement panels and white corrugated metal clad the building's exterior while the walls of the balconies and stairwell, visible from the street, are painted bright yellow, adding an attractive pop of color. Inside, pale wooden flooring is paired with white walls and simple lacquered cabinets to create a bright and airy atmosphere.

As with Tiny Tower, the building is centered around a vertical circulation program to maximize internal space. "Incorporating an elevator and two staircases would have left too little area for apartments," says Phillips, "so we strategized the tallest walk-up building with a single stair. Mezzanine levels further increased the floor space while working within the constraints of wood-frame construction."

As their design and research prove, ISA's commitment to rethinking city living is at the forefront of their practice. As Phillips sees it, our urban reality has endured centuries of "war, pandemics, economic crashes, and natural disasters," he says. "Its resilience through history is evidence that cities will prevail as centers of political, social, and economic identities into the 21st century and beyond." ●

XS House
Innovative strategies that include facade projections extending out beyond the footprint and mezzanines within the apartments substantially increased

Six homes on the site of just one

- MISSING-MIDDLE INFILL HOUSING
- HAECCITY STUDIO ARCHITECTURE
- VANCOUVER, CANADA

This densification project is located in a heritage neighborhood of Vancouver, where the majority of dwellings are of one-family ownership. So, it is with some sensitivity that the architects sought to introduce the concept of shared rental accommodation for several families on a single lot that was once occupied by a 1950s bungalow. One major consideration of the development is that there is no space for parking, as the accommodation is aimed at residents seeking a walkable urban lifestyle. In order to increase the favorability of the project further, the architects borrowed elements from the dominant heritage style, allowing the building to insert itself gently among the existing historical buildings. Its modern expression makes a deliberate nod to some of the more traditional typologies of the neighboring houses—the sloped roof, separate exterior dwelling entrances, and a network of intimate paths and walkways are just a few examples. The end result is a three-story walk-up, that offers six dedicated long-term units with a rooftop, green roof, and shared courtyard. As such, the project demonstrates that it is possible to achieve gentle densification that also respects neighboring architecture.

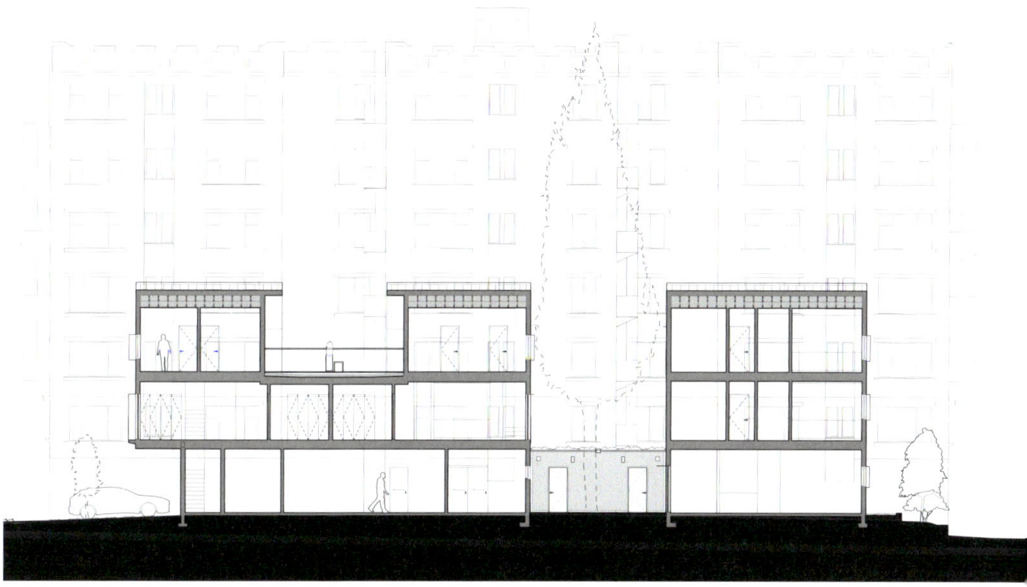

This multi-family rental project lies sandwiched between a seven-story heritage building on one side and a two-and-a-half story heritage house on the other.

A poetic response to an unusual brief

- HAFFENDEN HOUSE
- PARA PROJECT
- SYRACUSE, NY, USA

Nothing about this building is as it first seems. Apparently dwarfed by its more traditional, clapboard neighbors, the interiors, in fact, feel spacious. The eastern, or rear, elevation reveals the generous proportions of the library-study on the second floor, seen through a gigantic picture window. The parabola-shaped ceiling of this room dips down alarmingly low to make space for a reading area below the roof—an unconventional attic illuminated only by small openings in the facade.

This is a writing studio for a couple—both poets—who live in an adjacent house. Amid their books is a singular theatrical feature: a large bathtub, sunk directly into the library floor. It looks out over the rear of the property, continuing the commitment to seclusion and reflection, even in a suburban setting. The opaque street-facing facade adds to this project's air of mystery; a silicone-impregnated translucent "skin" covers the surface and shields the inhabitants from prying eyes.

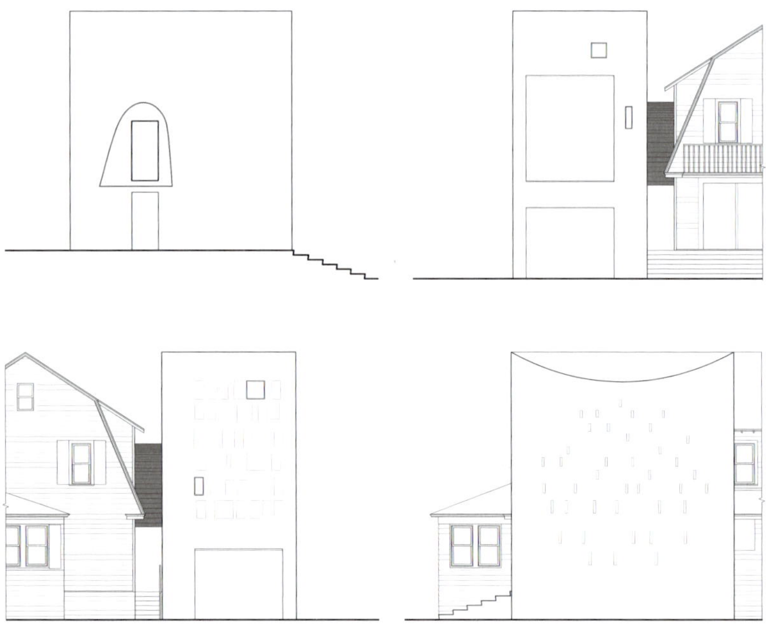

Inside and out, with the exception of minimal furnishings and the spines of the books on the shelves, the slim volume is predominantly white—a calming backdrop for quiet contemplation and creativity.

Healing SCARchitecture

- SKINNYSCAR
- GWENDOLYN HUISMAN & MARIJN BOTERMAN
- ROTTERDAM, NETHERLANDS

In the narrow Schoonoordstraat in Rotterdam's Oude Noorden neighborhood, a small overlooked site had sat vacant since the 1980s. Husband-and-wife duo, architects Gwendolyn Huisman and Marijn Boterman saw this as an opportunity to explore the possibilities of infill architecture in their city. "It was an overgrown patch of green, hidden behind a tall wooden fence," the architects recall.

Boterman previously worked with JagerJanssen Architecten and was aware of the firm's work in mapping out narrow, vacant lots in Rotterdam, including this one, labeling them as scars in the urban fabric that were in need of "healing." The couple approached the firm to develop said lot as SkinnySCAR—formerly known as SCAR #19. The SCARchitecture initiative aims to re-densify downtown Rotterdam, which is currently facing a housing shortage. "These gaps can be upgraded to complete the urban fabric," Huisman and Boterman say, "while giving it a boost and creating possibilities for new forms of urban living for the adventurous ones."

In 2016, Huisman and Boterman set up camp in the backyard of the 753-square-foot (70-square-meter) site. The plot's narrow dimensions "resulted in a stacked open loft typology," Huisman and Boterman say of their three-level home, which uses cement load-bearing slabs at its center. This design allows structurally for spacious volumes and large, unobstructed windows. In a nod to the neighboring houses—mostly late 19th to early 20th century buildings—the south facade uses black brick with a diamond-shaped pattern at the top.

To maintain the open plan and maximize a total of 1,507 square feet (140 square meters), the architects decided on a central utility core boxed in around the load-bearing concrete structure. The kitchen, bathrooms, and all storage are concealed within the plywood-clad core, leaving all walls bare and painted white. No space is spared in said core, whether it's used for open shelves on the first two floors or wooden storage cabinets that open onto the stairs.

The staircase wraps around the core with see-through risers that enhance communication between floors. The entrance hall guides the visitor all the way through to the open kitchen and dining area and out toward the garden, where glass doors fold out to the sides and make the space even more ample. Above the dining area, "a void in the living room connects the ground floor with the first level." The architects covered the void with a rope netting that provides a playful lounging area, acting as a built-in hammock.

The architects focused on using sustainable energy and materials throughout the house. They wanted to minimize their environmental impact, both during construction and long-term, while living in the house. They also chose to leave most materials in their rough state, from the pine plywood to the site-cast concrete floors. "Rust stains on the concrete ceiling are a remembrance of the wet season in which they were cast," say Huisman and Boterman, who were not looking for pristine conditions.

The interiors are meticulously orchestrated with clever built-in storage solutions and exquisite finishes; concrete floors remain raw on the ceiling side—a reminder of their construction.

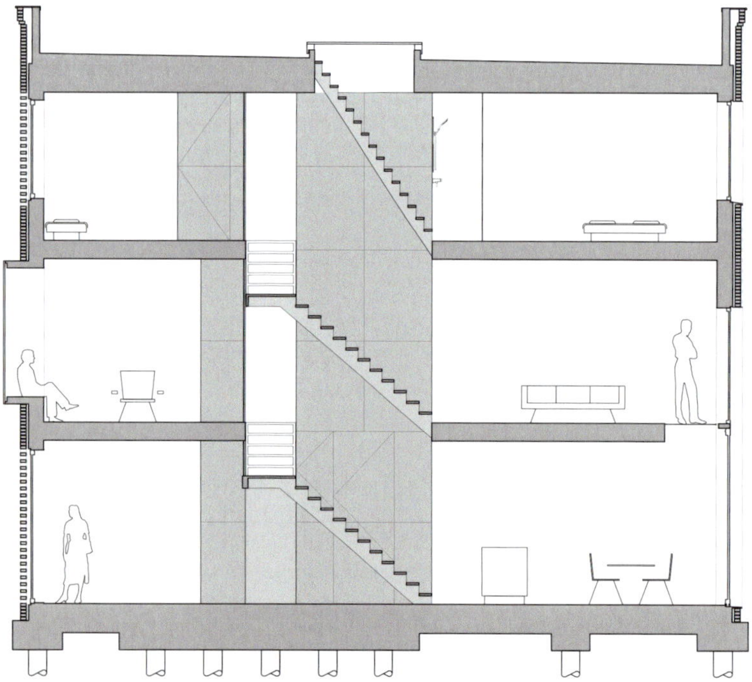

With its two-story window, the rear of the house is in stark contrast to the more closed facade facing the street; a skylight above the bathtub brings natural daylight into the darker zone of the house.

Site-specific design taken to the extreme

- ACUTE HOUSE
- OOF! ARCHITECTURE
- MELBOURNE, AUSTRALIA

A truly original project that has replaced the pre-existing building on site—a derelict white clapboard house that was something of a neighborhood landmark—and regurgitated it as a modern family home. In addition to familiar energy-saving features such as double-paned windows, insulation, and the use of high-efficiency appliances, the old cottage itself has been cannibalized for every material, from warped clapboards and fence slats to doorknobs. Reused and remounted, these elements take on a new life.

The architects describe this project as very specific to its context, highlighting the importance of renovating "weird 'leftover' sites" in the densely urbanized city of Melbourne. This house sits on a narrow, triangular plot, and some clever strategies have been employed to maximize space: a triangular staircase, open-plan floor layouts, and no corridors. With not a scrap of outdoor space, however, some eccentric touches bring the outdoors in: an aquarium, lawn-green carpets, and expansive views from every room.

Previous pages
The facades of Acute House juxtapose powder-coated aluminum panels with weatherboarding that was salvaged from a Victorian cottage that once inhabited the site.

Current pages
With the open staircase situated in the tightest cornerof the house, the "wedge-shaped" living spaces are designed to offer multiple overlapping uses.

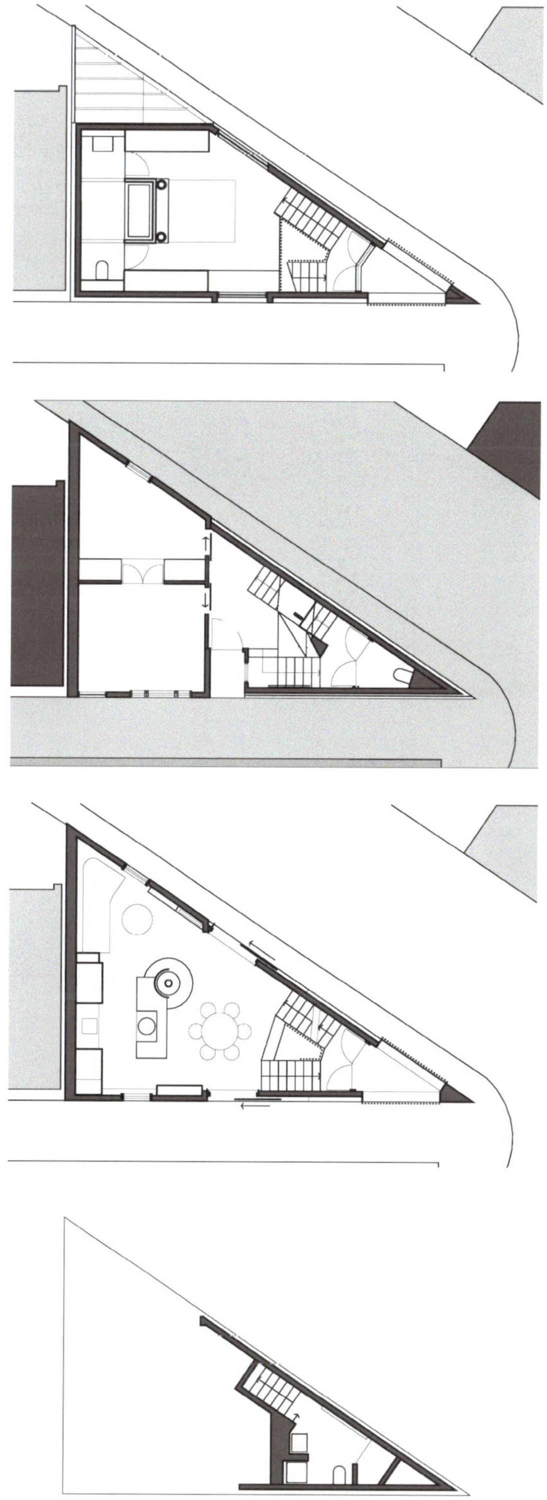

This page
Internal finishes feature commonly available sustainable materials such as plantation-grown Australian hardwoods, plywood, and recycled timber cladding with minimal painting.

Opposite
The floor plans show how the rooms on each floor are oriented to best suit their purpose, functionality, and needs.

A house like a Twitter feed

- TSUBOMI HOUSE
- YOSHINORI SAKANO ARCHITECTS
- TOKYO, JAPAN

With seven levels—each one small, but completely open—connected by a central staircase, the appearance of this house changes quickly and completely with every step upwards, and the effect is somewhat disorientating. The architect likens the rapid series of small gestures to online activity, and especially the brief messages on Twitter. The experience of social media, where individuals share and communicate information online, is also reflected in the overall concept of a family home with one communal space and no private rooms.

The idea is austere, but the execution, as the name of the home—"Bud House," in English—suggests, is intended to be intimate and comforting, as if the building were an unopened flower, tucked away in the city. The parallelogram-shaped larch ply panels that line the internal space are arranged in a chevron pattern that is echoed on the external facade. It is a warm treatment that is only abandoned in the lower, sunken levels, accessed by visitors to the ground-floor candy shop.

Previous pages
The two views of the exterior show how the house is sandwiched into a corner space between the buildings that flank it on either side.

Current pages
The "seven" levels are deceptive, as some spaces have double or triple height ceilings.

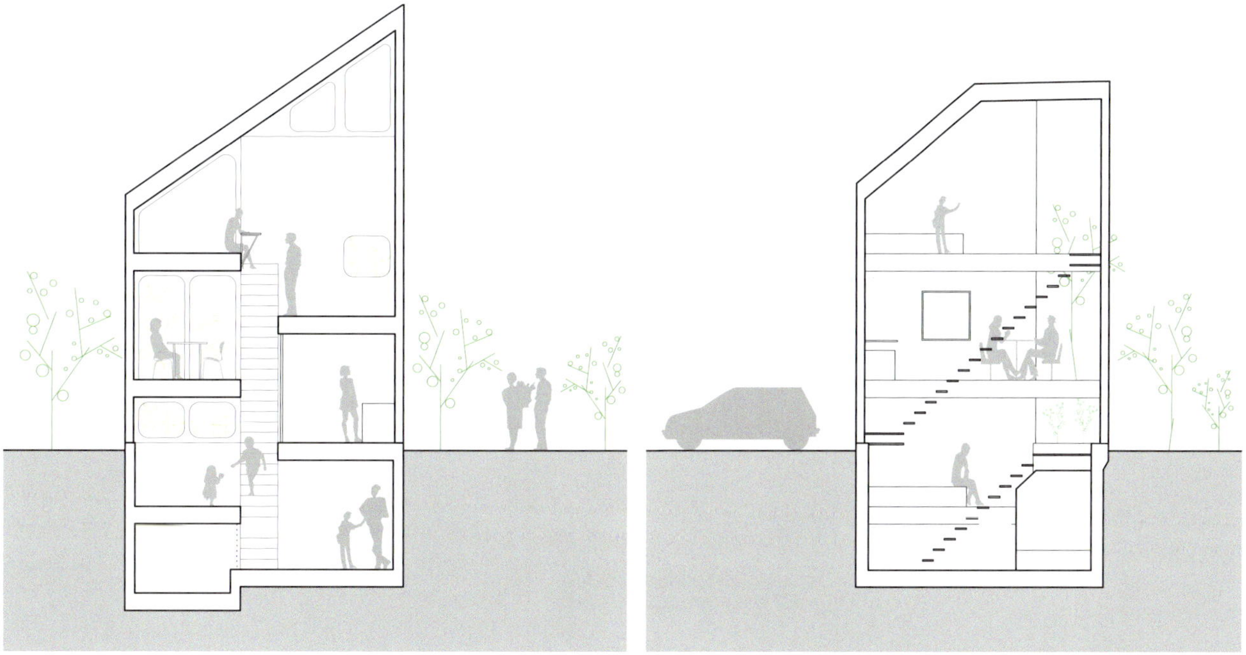

The house is a riot of angles, from the chevron ply to the windows that look out over the street and the creative spaces forged by the zigzagging stairs.

A machine for living in Lisbon

- DODGED HOUSE
- BUREAU
- LISBON, PORTUGAL

Unlike most of the projects presented in this book, this dwelling seems to buck the current trends. Instead of squeezing function and efficiency into every available corner of the building, Bureau have squandered half of the available space, having allocated it to a void that is four stories tall. What's left remains almost brutally functional—this really is a machine for living in the purest sense. Accessed via a spiral staircase in one corner of the room, each floor of the house overhangs the one immediately below it. The floors step out in this way as they rise up the building, with each end wall a single sheet of reinforced glass, so that the occupants of all rooms overlook the void that dominates the dwelling. The name, Dodged House, alludes to American architect Irving Gill's Dodge House in California, which combined modernism with elements borrowed from the architecture of the Spanish missions. Similarly, here, the architects have concealed their minimalist home behind a replica of a period facade in Lisbon.

Previous pages
From the street onlookers gain no impression of the unconventional layout beyond the facadc. All but one of its windows is filled in.

Current pages
The building uses standard materials and construction methods to reduce the overall cost—cement block walls over a reinforced concrete frame.

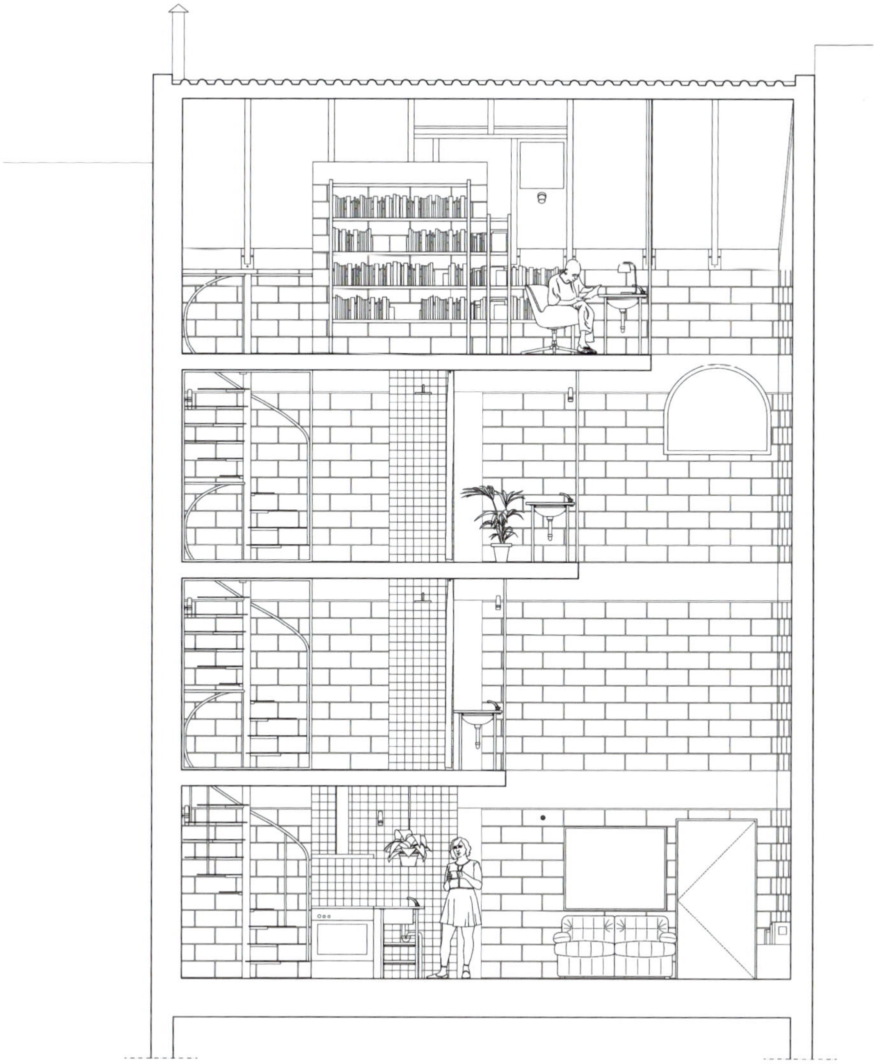

With the exception of a few pieces of wooden furniture, the home's fixtures and fittings are predominantly white, as are the concrete walls, which have been painted to brighten the interior.

The rear facade of the house, painted white, has a series of arched windows, one above the other. Below, a cobbled courtyard functions as a calm and neutral space.

Warm minimalism in a vertical form

- SKINNY HOUSE
- OLIVER DU PUY ARCHITECTS
- MELBOURNE, AUSTRALIA

From the street, Skinny House in Melbourne has an almost monastic aesthetic. A bare off-form concrete cross stands as if the structure is unfinished or left exposed and subject to the elements. However, the open structure of the facade is far from accidental: it is through this symmetrical framework that the spaces inside the 14-foot-wide (4.2-meter-wide) minimalist building are delineated. The architect, Oliver du Puy, established his design practice in 2015 after training in the Tokyo offices of architects Kengo Kuma and Junya Ishigami. In Japan he gained experience in Japanese concepts such as *shinrin-yoku,* or "forest bathing," a nature therapy that calls for constant human contact with the outdoors. "Light is used as a mediator between space and form," du Puy says, "to change the expression of the interior with time, and in so doing, connect the occupant with nature." The owner, "a high-frequency trader, atheist, and keen meditator," wanted a second home to which he could seasonally retire from his hectic lifestyle in London.

Working with simple, high-quality materials in their natural state—oak, stainless steel, and Tinos Verde and Carrara marble, sourced from Greece and Italy, respectively—du Puy transformed a former "rear yard of a 19th-century Victorian shop" into a haven for introspection. He used precise orientation to direct natural light into each room, informed by the daily rituals of the resident. The "transient nature of light guides the passing of time as it comes in contact with the materials," du Puy notes.

The singular site of 968 square feet (90 square meters) is devoid of any reminders of confinement because of the use of open spaces, which are imbued with a sense of poetry. A constant rhythm of light and shadow "paint" the walls as the day passes by. The spaces facing north along the two-story house are "structured like a haiku poem," du Puy notes, "a suite of intimate moments increasing in privacy as one ascends the building." Carefully chosen furniture by London-based designer Faye Toogood provides sculptural accents, and the 1972 classic leather bed by Mario Bellini seems right at home on the top floor.

White walls and perfectly polished concrete floors contribute to the feeling of openness, which is further enhanced by skylights and floor-to-ceiling windows. An enclosed garden covered with white gravel on the ground floor, as well as the gauzy drapery and textured rugs on the first and second levels, add a cozy ambiance to the otherwise bare, almost clinical, styling. Likewise, the wood-framed windows contrast with the stainless-steel railing used on the balconies, creating a warm refuge to wind down after hectic days at the trading desk.

Previous pages
The street facade of the building recedes as the floors ascend, affording the uppermost rooms the greatest privacy.

Current pages
A tranquil courtyard and verdant views to the rear of the house allow the inhabitants to feel immersed in nature.

Soft polished concrete, natural textures, and neutral textiles contribute to the deep sense of calm that pervades the house.

Surrounded by neighbors, an island of calm

- SHOEI HOUSE
- HEARTH ARCHITECTS
- SHIGA, JAPAN

This house, situated on a plot that measures 18 feet (5.5 meters) wide and 104 feet (32 meters) long has the "eel's nest" proportions of many city-center homes in traditional Japanese cities, but its quiet simplicity sets it apart from other, more structurally inventive takes on the form (see page 206).

Overlooked on all sides, but especially on the north and south (long) elevations, the residents' privacy was prioritized by placing bedrooms on the ground level and shielding them from view, while the main living spaces are arranged over the floor above. Even there, the windows on the street-facing facade are relatively small, or covered by wooden screens, and the primary light sources are the skylights. At either end of the building, there are larger apertures beside semi-enclosed verandas with delicate planting. The potential drawbacks of this scheme are sidestepped by features that draw light into the interior and amplify it—high ceilings and the use of pale timber throughout—or with elements, such as pools of artificial light, that simply make a virtue of its absence.

Previous pages
The site is six times longer than it is wide. The architects have exploited this to allow for a sizeable garden at the entrance to the house.

Current pages
The interior and exterior spaces complement each other, both having rendered walls, timber elements, and plenty of greenery.

Most of the natural light enters the building through the windows at the gable ends and via a skylight; windows down the length of the building feature privacy screens.

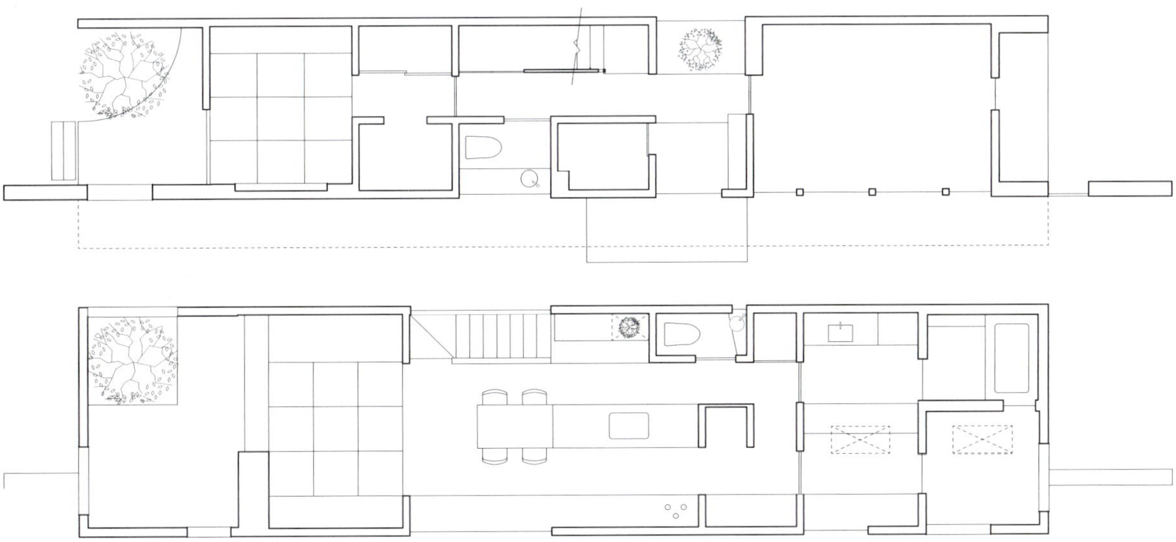

INDEX

Vertical Living
Compact Architecture for Urban Spaces

This book was conceived, edited, and designed by gestalten.

Edited by Robert Klanten and Elli Stuhler

Foreword by Chris Precht
Profile, Case Study, and Feature texts by Natalia Torija
Project texts by Faye Robson

Editorial Management by Adam Jackman and Sam Stevenson

Design and Layout by Ilona Samcewicz-Parham

Photo Editors: Valentina Marinai and Mario Udzenija

Typeface: La Nord by Raoul Gottschling

Cover photography by Takumi Ota
Backcover images by Timothy Soar (top),
Takumi Ota (middle left), Åke E:son Lindman (middle right),
Courtesy of Yoshinori Sakano Architects (middle right)

Printed by Grafisches Centrum Cuno GmbH & Co. KG, Calbe
Made in Germany

Published by gestalten, Berlin 2021
ISBN 978-3-89955-871-5

Bibliographic information published by the Deutsche Nationalbibliothek.
The Deutsche Nationalbibliothek lists this publication in the Deutsche Nationalbibliografie; detailed bibliographic data is available online at www.dnb.de

None of the content in this book was published in exchange for payment by commercial parties or designers; gestalten selected all included work based solely on its artistic merit.

This book was printed on paper certified according to the standards of the FSC®.

FSC www.fsc.org MIX Paper from responsible sources FSC® C043106